"FLOWER GARDEN"
33" x 33"
by Lori Simpson, Olathe, KS, 2004

"RAIL FENCE A BLOOMIN'"
37 1/2" x 50 1/2"
by Kathy Delaney, Overland Park, KS, quilted by Martha Heimbaugh, 2003

THE BASICS

An Easy Guide to Beginning Quiltmaking

By Kathy Delaney

KANSAS CITY STAR BOOKS

ACKNOWLEDGEMENTS

First I'd like to thank Doug Weaver for having the confidence in me to ask me to write this book. I have thoroughly enjoyed this challenge!

I thank my mother, Vi Berry, for instilling in me the love of fabric. With her guidance, I have been fondling fabric and wrangling sewing machines since I was a very little girl. With her teaching, I became skilled enough to make all of my own clothes by the time I was 12. While she never had introduced me to quilts, Mother has been by best buddy in this endeavor since we went to our first AQS quilt show together in Paducah, Kentucky in 1997. She never laughed when I dreamed out loud, "Someday I'm going to have a quilt exhibited here!"

I thank Rich, my husband, and Sean and Ian, my sons, for encouraging me and appreciating the quilts.

I thank my employer and friend, Carol Kirchhoff, owner of Prairie Point Quilts in Shawnee, Kansas for her support and encouragement in all of my projects. I'd also like to thank all of my co-workers at Prairie Point for their encouragement and letting me bounce ideas around them. Without them I might have never covered all the bases!

I thank Jeanne Poore for her encouragement and for rescuing me when my brain freezes and the numbers just don't want to make any sense. She always seems to know the answers to my questions.

I thank my friend and fellow guild member, Lori Simpson, for testing my patterns from the beginning quilter's viewpoint. Lori, with other members of the Olathe Quilter's Guild, has offered some of the most valuable suggestions.

I thank Linda Mooney for her enthusiasm for this project. Her samples in the gallery, along with all the others, serve as inspiration for all of us.

I thank Judy Pearlstein for her hard work editing these pages. She kept me on track! A big thank you goes to Vicky Frenkel for designing a very usable book. She made my imagination come to life! A grateful thank you to JoAnn Groves for the hard work she put in on making the instructional photographs look right. I'd like to say thank you to Bill Krzyzanowski for his inspiring photographs. His skill and creativity make the quilts come alive on the page!

And last, but by no means least, I thank you, the reader, for buying this book. I hope this is the beginning of a wonderful journey for you and that you love making quilts as much as I do!

THE BASICS,
An Easy Guide to Quiltmaking

by Kathy Delaney

Editor: Judy Pearlstein
Design: Vicky Frenkel
Photography: Bill Krzyzanowski
Production Assistance: JoAnn Groves
Instructional photos and graphics by Kathy Delaney
Sewing machine courtesy of Betty Becker
"Sampler" fabric is Bukhara from Maywood Studios

Published by Kansas City Star Books
1729 Grand Blvd., Kansas City, Missouri, 64108
All rights reserved
Copyright© 2004 by The Kansas City Star Co.

First edition

Printed in the United States of America by Walsworth Publishing Co.

To order copies, call StarInfo (816-234-4636)

www.PickleDish.com

TABLE OF CONTENTS

ABOUT THE AUTHOR

Kathy cannot remember exactly when she began sewing but she can remember her first sewing machine. It was a toy that actually sewed and she made crude clothing for her dolls. Eventually she graduated to her mother's Feather Weight and then to her mother's new Singer. (Unfortunately the Feather Weight was traded in for the new machine at a time when Singer was destroying the old to make way for the new!) Eventually Kathy graduated from very simple clothing to tailored coats for herself and suits for her husband. But in 1991 she met her first quilt and can count on one hand the number of garments she has made in the years since!

Since playing school at a very young age (her dolls and dog were her students), Kathy has been a teacher. She loves sharing what she knows with anyone who wishes it. What better venue to share quiltmaking knowledge than teaching quilt groups around the country and writing books about quiltmaking? Next to actually making quilts, Kathy's favorite activity is teaching others to make quilts.

Kathy lives in Overland Park, Kansas with Rich Delaney, her husband of 34 years. At this writing, her older son, Sean, is a member of the United States Army and is in Baghdad. Her younger son, Ian, is a member of the Arizona Repertory Theater at the University of Arizona where he is in the acting program.

THE BASICS

AN EASY GUIDE TO BEGINNING QUILTMAKING

Introduction

You love quilts! Maybe your grandmother or mother made quilts and, as a young child, you watched them work. Maybe you have a friend who makes quilts and you have admired her work and thought to yourself that she must have some special talent, and you wish you, too, could make quilts. Maybe your new sister-in-law dragged you to a quilt show and you saw your first quilt and fell in love.

It doesn't matter what your reasons, you just know that you are ready to make a quilt. You have come to the right place! This book is for you, the brand new quilter. I'm going to explain tools as well as techniques that will get you started in your quiltmaking career. The 16 blocks of the Sampler quilt will give you very basic techniques in quiltmaking and a very solid foundation, preparing you for many quilts to come. The rest of the projects are designed to give you a good solid background as you progress to more complicated patterns.

Within the pages of this book, we will go step by step from buying the fabric for your first quilt, to gathering the tools you will need, all the way to placing a label on the back of your first finished quilt. Together we will make a quilter out of you and you will find a life-long passion that only gets better and stronger over time. Are you ready for some fun? Me, too!

4

CHAPTER 1
LET'S BEGIN WITH THE FABRIC AND TOOLS

FABRIC

Traditionally, quilts are made with 100% cotton fabric. Your local quilt store is brimming with quality fabrics in a myriad of colors, prints, and visual textures. The first step is to find what you like. Some quilters think that choosing the fabric for their quilt is the hardest part. Actually, today that's one of the easiest parts! There are so many companies now that are making literally thousands of different fabrics each, that you can't help but find a great combination for your quilt. Good advice is to purchase the best fabric that you can afford. Your quilt will hold up better to use and washings if you use a good, quilt-shop quality 100% cotton fabric.

Color

Let's take a quick look at color. If you don't have a colorwheel, you might want to either get one from an art store, or you can quickly draw one of your own.

Begin with an equilateral triangle. At each point, assign a primary color: red, yellow and blue.

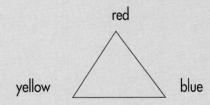

Now place another triangle over the first and add the secondary colors violet (between the red and blue), green (between the yellow and blue) and orange (between the red and yellow).

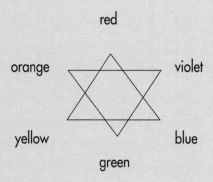

The last step is to add spokes and the tertiary colors red-violet (between the red and violet), blue-violet (between the blue and violet), blue-green (between the blue and green), yellow-green (between yellow and green), yellow-orange (between the yellow and orange) and red-orange (between the red and orange).

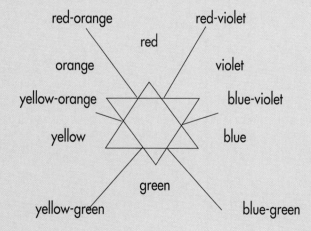

Now you're all set to answer any color question you have. I think the most common question is, "What colors go together?" By arranging colors into a color scheme, you'll be on your way.

The most restful and safe color scheme is monochromatic. This is one color. A variety of fabrics all the same color, such as all blue, are a very popular combination. Just make sure that no one fabric stands out as if it doesn't belong. Use a variety of light blues, medium blues and dark blues, but you might consider leaving out the one very bright, intense blue if you're using a lot of soft, country blues. Either leave it out or give it plenty of company by adding more. Print is important, too. Combine large prints with small prints and stripes and plaids. It would be boring to use all small prints or all large prints. A variety is much more interesting.

A two-color quilt is very traditional. Red and white or blue and white are very striking and very traditional. The contrast between the color and the white are very exciting to the eye.

Now, let's go back to your color wheel and make up some formulas. Colors opposite each other on the color wheel are called complementary, such as red and green, or blue and orange or yellow-green and red-violet. You have to be careful with this scheme because you can get into trouble.

Sometimes they want to fight. But, how about the two colors on either side of the one opposite? This is a split complementary and can be quite interesting: Red, yellow-green and blue-green or yellow-green, yellow-orange and violet, for instance.

If you superimpose geometric shapes on your color wheel you can combine those colors into a quilt. A triangle, three colors equidistant from each other, would look nice. A square, four colors equidistant from each other, works well, too. Try a rectangle. See where I'm going? A little geometry and your color wheel and you can't go wrong. By the way, using all the colors is called polychromatic. A polychromatic quilt, sometimes called a scrap quilt, is probably the least difficult to organize. There is no need for matching since you will be using all the colors. But you might want to save that quilt until you have some scraps. Trying to buy the smallest amount, usually 1/8 yard, of 100 fabrics or more can get quite expensive. Trust me, before very long, you will have a stash, or collection of fabric, without even trying!

Another way to choose your fabrics is to find one print that has five or more colors that you really like. This is called your focus fabric. Then choose more fabrics that are the same as those colors. (You'll find little color dots in the selvage, or one edge, of the printed fabric that show you what colors are in the print.) The quilt pattern that you choose will guide you in regard to the number of different fabrics you'll need for your quilt. The patterns in this book will clearly tell what you need and how much you'll use.

Speaking of the amount of fabric you'll need: some pattern designers figure the amounts down to the inch. You'll want to buy an extra 1/4 or 1/3 yard, depending on the patch sizes in your blocks just in case there is a mistake, either in the pattern or your cutting. Some designers add an extra 1/4 yard to each amount automatically "just in

case." The clerk at the quilt shop should be able to help you determine what the designer has done. The patterns in this book have an extra 1/4 yard added if warranted. You should not run short. And there is a rule that every quilter lives by - "You can never have too much fabric!" No one wants to run out of a particular fabric when they just have one or two more blocks to make to finish the quilt top. Chances are, when you go back for that little bit that you need, the fabric will no longer be available! It truly is a good idea to buy a little extra. You can always use the extra to piece together to create the backing of the quilt.

Fabric width seems to fluxuate from generation to generation. When I was making clothing as a kid in the 1960's, fabric was 35" wide. As an adult I found that fabric grew to 44"-45" wide. Now, it seems, fabric is on the way back down.

Often you'll find fabric is just 40" wide. If you wash the fabric before you use it, a 44" wide fabric could shrink to 41" wide or even less. And on the long edges of the fabric is a 1/2" wide selvage that should not be used because the weave of the fabric is tighter than the main body. So, once you have removed the selvage, the usable fabric shrinks to 40" wide. When I calculate the amount of fabric I'm going to need, I calculate it based on 40" of usable width no matter what the actual width.

The clerks at your local quilt shop will be able to help you and would love to do it. When we help a quilter choose her fabrics, we feel very satisfied. That's one less quilt we have to make!

To wash or not to wash, that is the question!

At the quilt shop where I work and at quilt guild meetings where I teach, I am often asked whether one should pre-wash the fabric before making it into a quilt. I always answer in the same way. "Those of us who work in a quilt shop will always tell you that you should wash your fabric. With that said, though, I don't always." Now that sounds pretty ambiguous and it is meant to.

I will always wash all the flannels I buy before making it into a quilt, as well as homespun fabrics. These fabrics often shrink and, unfortunately, not at a uniform rate. I want the shrinkage out of the way before I make the quilt. Unfortunately there are some fabrics that will shrink that are not homespun or flannel. Testing for shrinkage is a good idea. If there is going to be shrinkage, you want it uniform. So washing before use is suggested. I will suggest that you always test your dark fabrics to see if they are going to bleed later. If in doubt, go ahead and wash it. There are some fabrics that are notorious bleeders and I just choose not to buy those. There are some fabrics that never seem to bleed and I don't bother washing those.

Some quilters will tell you that washing fabric that you plan to use in an appliqué project will relax the fabric and make the fabric easier to manipulate. Personally, most of the time I find no difference. If it's really stiff from heavy dye or sizing, I probably won't buy the fabric unless it is absolutely perfect! Some quilters will tell you that not washing the fabric with which you plan to piece will maintain the sizing and make piecing easier. There are some

patterns for which I'll even add starch to the finish to aid in the piecing. You will read the following words often in this book. "You are going to have to test the different methods and decide what works best for you!" I don't think anyone can give you exact rules to go by every time! But if in doubt, prewash!

By the way, prewashing the fabric will cause the fabric to ravel. The raveled edge can easily be removed when you begin to cut your strips or blocks, but that raveling sure can cause havoc when trying to separate the pieces after washing. The raveling also tightens the wrinkles and it is harder to press the fabric smooth. I eliminate the raveling in one of two ways. Either I sew the raw edges, that is the cut edges, with a zigzag stitch on my sewing machine or I sew the edge with my serger machine, a machine that finishes the raw edges of my fabric with an overlocking stitch. I still have to trim those edges, but I don't have the tied mess of fabric that I would otherwise after washing and drying. By the way, the serger is by no means necessary to quilt making. If you have one it is likely because you construct garments. Don't go out and buy one to make quilts. You would not use it to piece your quilt tops.

Mattress sizes — quilt sizes

In deciding the size of the quilt you want to make, there are many variables to consider. There are industry-wide mattress surface sizes but each manufacturer then has its own idea of how deep the mattress should be. The coverings of the mattress, the interior padding, the interior springs all contribute to the depth of the mattress. You will need to measure your mattress to determine the correct quilt size for your bed. Following you will find a guide. If your mattress is deeper, you will need to increase the size of the quilt accordingly, but the list below will get you started. By the way, the drop is the distance from the edge of the mattress, down the side to the outer edge of the quilt.

Twin mattress: 39" x 75"
Twin quilt with 12" drop on all 4 sides: 63" x 99"
Double mattress: 54" x 75"
Double quilt with 12" drop on all 4 sides: 78" x 99"
Queen mattress: 60" x 80"
Queen quilt with 12" drop on all 4 sides: 84" x 104"
King mattress: 76" x 80"
King quilt with 12" drop on all 4 sides: 100" x 104"

Should you wish to allow for a pillow tuck, consider adding to the length of the quilt. An additional row or two of blocks, depending on their size, may be all you need.

TOOLS OF THE CRAFT

Sewing machine

As a beginning quilter, chances are you have picked up a few of the magazines dedicated to the art of making quilts to dream a little and see if you can find out how to make a quilt. You have probably noticed the ads for the wonderful new sewing machines that do almost everything but cook your family's dinner! There are so many wonderful machines made now. Each one will offer different features and you'll just have to go try them all out to determine the best one for you.

I have quilting friends who sew on state-of-the-art machines and I have quilting friends who wouldn't sew on anything but their more-than-50-year-old Singer Featherweight and still others who sew on everything in between. All you need is an even straight stitch, a reverse stitch and a way to determine a 1/4" seam allowance. Other helpful features include an even feed or walking foot and a free motion foot. Everything else is extra - fun, but extra.

If you are in the market to buy a new machine, be sure to take along some of your own fabric to test the machines' sewing abilities. I found that the fabric the sewing companies use for demonstrating are heavily starched and really do not reflect my sewing habits. I think the sewing experiences are not at all realistic so that once I get the new machine home, nothing seems as it did in the store.

One of the most important things you can do as a new quilter is to become very friendly with your machine. Read the owner's manual. If you have received a hand-me-down and did not also receive this valuable booklet, contact your machine's manufacturer and see about obtaining a new one.

Sewing machine needles

When you go to your favorite sewing center for sewing

machine needles, you are, more than likely, going to be greeted with a very large selection of different machine needles. (We won't even mention the hand sewing needles at this time!) Trying to decide which ones to buy can be quite confusing. Each needle package will have a pair of numbers. The first number in the pair will refer to the European metric system that indicates the diameter of the shaft. The smaller this number, the smaller the needle size. The second number is the American needle size. To make it really confusing, this number is not related to the actual physical size of the needle or the eye, but the larger number indicates the larger needles.

I have found that a majority of my students just settle for the "Universal" needles. After all, "universal" sounds like it will work for any machine and any project! Right? In theory, that sounds good. However, the variety of needles is actually manufactured for a reason.

While the Universal needle will work for most of your quilting needs, there are aspects of it that may not. Two of the most important aspects to consider when choosing your needle are the eye of the needle and the point of the needle. The eye has to be the correct size to fit your thread and the point has to penetrate the fabric correctly.

Along the shaft of the needle, above the eye and leading to the eye, is a groove that the thread lies in as it travels along the shaft. This groove is important to the size of your thread. A thicker thread will not fit the narrower groove and smaller eye and your stitches won't be even. Likewise, a very thin thread will not lie in the wider groove

and larger eye, making your stitches uneven.

For piecing cotton patches with 50 weight cotton thread, I usually use the Universal needle size 80/12 or the Quilting needle size 80/12. The point of the Universal is slightly rounded while the point of the Quilting needle is very sharp. While you would not want to use a blunt or really rounded needlepoint for your woven fabric, the slightly rounded feature of the Universal will work.

For paper foundation piecing I use the Universal needle size 90/14. The eye of this sized needle is larger so the shaft of the needle is a little larger. It will perforate my paper foundation so that removing it later is easier.

For quilting by machine I use the Quilting needle size 80/12. This needle is very sharp and will make a smaller hole in the fabric. The thread from the bobbin is less likely to escape through the hole and show on top.

If I am using a metallic thread, I use a Metafil or Metallica needle. The eye is coated with a Teflon-like material so that the metallic thread won't get hung up and break. When sewing with a metallic thread, be sure to sew slower.

For other specialized sewing projects, you might check with the sales help in your sewing center for recommendations regarding needle choice.

With all the different types of needles you'll be using, you might find it hard to tell which needle is which once they are out of the package and which needle is in the machine! The needles themselves do have the size marked on the shaft but it takes a microscope to be able to read it! I don't know where I heard the following tip so I cannot give credit to someone, but I didn't come up with it and I think it is brilliant. The "tomato" pincushions are segmented with seams or sometimes cording. With a permanent marker, mark each segment a different needle type and size. You will know exactly what you have stored there for later use. And if you put a sticky note on your machine with the needle type and size you are currently using,

you will know which segment to store it in when you change needles. Speaking of changing needles, it is advised that you begin each new project with a new needle.

Thread

When sewing cotton quilting fabric, plan to use cotton thread. There are a number of manufacturers and I think every quilter probably has her favorite. The sewing machine manufacturers also seem to have their favorites, but for different reasons. The sewing machine manufacturers want you to use thread that will not create so much dust. The dust builds up in the machine and tends to "gum up the works."

Some very inexpensive threads, while marked as cotton, have other characteristics that both quilters and machine manufacturers, alike, want to avoid. Some of these threads have tiny knots that connect lengths of thread into one entire spool. These knots can cause problems, from breaking while you are stitching to throwing the tension out of whack in the machine.

I have two suggestions. One is to remember that you get what you pay for. If you've bought thread from the bin marked "4 spools for $1", you might be buying much more expensive trouble. My other suggestion is to check with the manufacturer of your sewing machine to see what they recommend. Paying a little more for the thread may save you lots of machine repair bills in the long run.

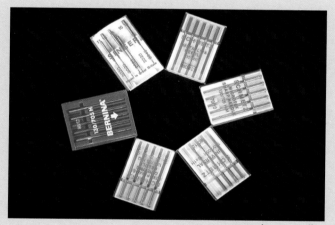

Machine needles

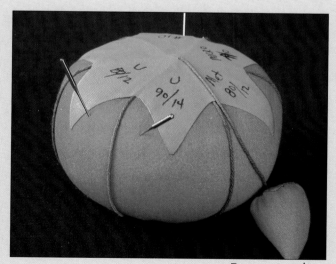

Tomato pincushion

Now, thread for appliqué and hand piecing is a different matter. I am partial to silk thread when I appliqué or an embroidery cotton for either appliqué or hand piecing. When I say embroidery cotton, I don't mean embroidery floss that you buy by the skein. Thread designed for the sewing machine that has the ability to make embroidered motifs is a finer thread than what you use for machine piecing. I use a 60-weight 2-ply machine embroidery cotton thread for hand piecing. If I cannot find the color I want in 50-weight silk for appliqué, I will use the machine embroidery cotton. I tend to stay away from the silk in hand piecing. It seems too slippery for me when I hand piece, although it's that slipperiness I love for appliqué!

1/4-inch foot

If your machine can accept one, a foot that is designed to guide the 1/4" seam allowance can be very handy. However, if you don't have one, or your machine won't accept one of the generic feet designed for this purpose, you can still make accurate 1/4" seam allowances. There are a variety of ways to mark the 1/4" on the sewing base of your machine.

Some quilters will purchase a foam pad from the foot ailment isle of the pharmacy. The pad is usually 1/8" thick or more and has a tackiness on one side to keep it in place. By cutting the pad so that it has a very straight edge, you can place the pad 1/4" from your needle position, taking care not to cover the feed dogs.

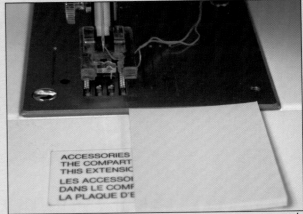

Post it notes as guide

Blue tape as guide

This will act as a "fence" along which you will guide your fabric as you sew. A short stack of sticky notes will do the same, although some quilters will stabilize the pad with a little tape.

You might also place a piece of blue painter's tape on the sewing base. The color of the tape makes it easy to see as you're sewing and the tape doesn't seem to leave the same residue as other masking tapes do.

Even-feed foot

As I mentioned previously, the even-feed foot is a beneficial addition to your machine. I use the even-feed if I am piecing a quilt with flannel fabrics as they have a little more give than regular cottons and tend to stretch. I also put bindings on with this foot. Since there are three layers of quilt and an additional two layers of binding, I want all the layers to feed as evenly as possible.

The even-feed foot has a set of feed dogs in the foot to match the movement of the feed dogs of the machine. This allows the bottom layer and the top layer of fabric to move along evenly.

Markers

At various times in the quiltmaking process you will find that you need to make marks on your fabric. Each job may require a different marker. In general, I use a light marker (such as soapstone, General's Chalk or Clover's gray mechanical pencil) on dark fabrics. In general, I use a dark marker (such as washable graphite, The Ultimate Marking Pencil or Clover's gray mechanical pencil) on light fabrics. Notice that Clover's gray mechanical pencil is listed for both light and dark fabric. This marker works for almost anything BUT gray or medium blue fabrics. I use the other markers instead.

It may be very important that the marker you use washes out of the fabric. There are times when the fabric will just not release the marker. Be sure you test the marker on the fabric before you use it, even if the marker is advertised as washable. You don't want a nasty surprise after your quilt is completed if you can avoid it just by a quick test.

Some quilters use a blue, water-soluble marker. A little water misted on the marker makes it seem to disappear. Even if you cannot see the mark, the chemical is still in your fabric. Be sure to wash the chemical from your fabric thoroughly. Never use hot water. Never iron the fabric with the marker still present. Never leave your marked quilt in a hot car. Heat will set the mark. Wash the quilt with cool water, soaking thoroughly and rinsing thoroughly before drying. And don't leave the marks in the quilt for too long a period. Time may set the marks as well. Humidity will remove the marks, too, but not the chemicals. Even if the marks disappear, you will need to wash the chemicals from your quilt. Did I mention that you must wash out the chemical from your quilt?

Some quilters like to use the purple marker that disap

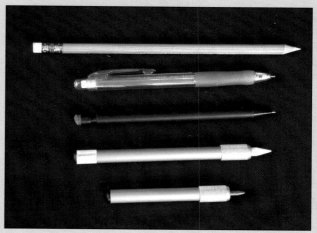

Fabric markers

pears into thin air. Again, the chemicals are still in the fabric. Be sure to wash out the marker, even if you cannot see the marks.

Pins

You'll want to use quilter's pins with a glass head so that an accidental touch by the iron will not melt the head of the pin. The glass head pins come in white, yellow and red. The red seem to be the thinnest but the white and yellow are good, too. I recommend that you use pins with the very thinnest shaft you can find. It makes pinning effortless. They are sharper than pins with a longer and thicker shaft. The round glass heads are smaller than the plastic allowing less distortion.

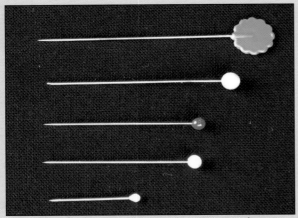

Quilters' pins

The tips are sharp and the heads don't seem to pull off of the shaft easily.

Rotary cutting tools

Once upon a time all cutting was done with scissors,

one patch at a time. And then in 1979 something monumental occurred. It was called the rotary cutter, a round razor blade that rolled through fabric, slicing the fabric as the blade rolled. The rotary cutter revolutionized quiltmaking!

Cutters

There are several good rotary cutters on the market. For every quilter, you are going to find a different favorite cutter. You'll need to take a look at them to compare. A good quilting supply store will let you try them out to see what feels good to you. I suggest that you don't consider anything smaller than a 45 mm blade to begin. The 60 mm blade will allow you to cut easily through more layers of fabric. But you probably won't need to worry about that. The 60 mm replacement blades can be quite expensive, too.

It is important that you remember that the rotary cutter can be very dangerous. Always retract the blade when you are not actually cutting. The blades are like razor blades. They are so sharp that you can cut a good chunk of finger off without even feeling it. Just a casual glancing blow to the open blade by the side of your hand can cause a great deal of damage. So, never set the cutter down without retracting the blade! Keep the hand securing the rotary cutting ruler well back from the cutting edge. And always wear shoes while you are using the rotary cutter. Dropping an open blade onto your foot can cause real damage!

If you have small children under foot, it is recommended

that you wait to do your rotary cutting until after the kids have gone down for a nap or are at a friend's house to play. You really don't need distractions while rotary cutting.

Your blade will stay sharp longer if you are careful NOT to hit pins or nick the side of your ruler with your cutter. There are sharpeners that you may purchase to give your cutter blades a new edge, extending the life of the blade. However, once there is a nick in the blade, the blade cannot be sharpened and needs to be replaced. (When discarding a blade, be sure to wrap it securely in the new blade's packaging before placing into the trash to keep anyone from getting hurt.) I recommend that you begin a new project with a new or newly sharpened blade. Over time the blade will become dull and cause damage to your mat. In addition, you have to work harder than you need.

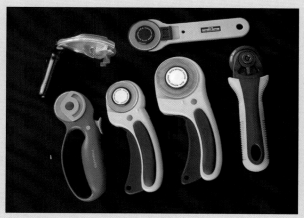

Rotary cutters

Check the nut that holds the whole mechanism together. If it is tightened too tightly, the blade will not rotate or roll easily through the fabric. The nut should be tight-

ened only until it meets resistance. A test to make sure the blade isn't too tightly secured is to hold the open cutter by the end of the handle with your finger tips. Push the cutter forward on your mat. Does the blade roll easily? Does it wobble? If the blade does not roll, loosen the nut just a little. If the blade wobbles, tighten the nut just a little.

Rulers

There are special rulers designed to work with rotary cutters. They are made of a sturdy acrylic that allows you to see the fabric beneath. You'll want a ruler with clear markings for measurements that include 1/8, 1/4, 1/2, 3/4, as well as inch markings. Rulers are available in all sorts of shapes and sizes. I recommend that you begin with a 6" x 24" and a 12 1/2" x 12 1/2". With these two rulers you can probably cut almost anything. Later you will find that a 6" x 12", a 6 1/2" x 6 1/2", a 9 1/2" x 9 1/2" and a 16" x 16" will come in handy, as well.

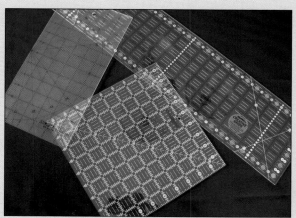

Rotary rulers

Later you will also find yourself investing in specialty rulers that will make quiltmaking easier and more enjoyable. There are rulers to cut triangles of all shapes, octagons, multiple strips and even curves. Quilters love new "toys", so keep your eyes open for special tools to do special projects.

Rotary cutting mats

The mat designed for rotary cutting is made of a material that is said to "self heal." This means that as you roll that very sharp rotary cutting blade over your mat, you will not be creating a permanent cut in the mat as well as your fabric. There are several companies that offer the mats. Each mat has different features to consider and they come in a variety of sizes. Some self heal more readily than others. I recommend for everyday use you purchase the largest mat you can afford.

No matter which one of the mats you choose, keep them stored flat and don't leave them for long periods in the extreme heat in your car. In other words, if you transport your mat in your car on a hot day, make sure that you keep it flat with nothing on top of it and take it indoors quickly. The mat will warp very easily. Once you put a curl in the mat, you can never get it out even if you try to leave it in the sun and then layer heavy books on top!

One side of the mat is usually marked with a grid while one side is usually blank. Many quilters are tempted to use the grid that is marked on the mat as a device to measure for each rotary cut. Because some grids can be inaccurate, I recommend that the grid be used for squaring the fabric only, never measuring it. If you cannot ignore the grid, consider turning over the mat and using the blank side.

Once your rotary cutter blade becomes dull, you will find that your mat begins to heal itself less. The dull blade forces tiny fibers from your fabric into the wound it creates in the mat, preventing the cut to heal. Those cuts then cause the rotary cutter to skip while cutting the fabric and you have to go back to release the missed threads. If your mat becomes very rough and you find lots of cuts, you can extend the life of the mat just by turning it over and using the other side. Another way to extend the life of the mat is to make sure that your rotary blades are not allowed to become dull.

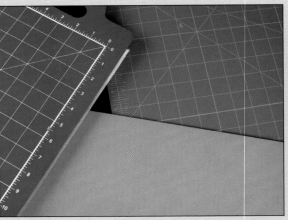

Rotary cutting mats

Scissors

Once upon a time there was one style of scissor: two knives that pivoted on a central screw with loops for your thumb and fingers. Today there are so many different styles that it is hard to say just which one a new quilter should have. I recommend that you have a pair of 8″ dressmaker style and a pair of 4″ embroidery scissors. After that I can't tell you which ones are the ones for you. You'll find scissors that are pretty hefty and some that are very light weight. You'll find scissors that are very sharp and will stay sharp for a very long time and you'll find scissors that will need regular sharpening. You'll find scissors that cost a small fortune and you'll find scissors that cost very little. The very nicest thing, though, is that you'll easily find scissors that are right for you!

Variety of scissors

CHAPTER 2
TECHNIQUES IN QUILTMAKING

ROTARY CUTTING

Before making your first cut in your fabric you will want to straighten it. This is easiest done if you've washed the fabric and pressed it. The original fold, from being rolled on to the bolt, will have disappeared and you'll be free to manipulate your fabric to create a new fold. Do not expect the fold that is in the fabric as you bring it home from your quilting supply store to be on the *straight of grain*. Most often it is not.

Before going any further, let me tell you a little about what straight of grain means. If you are at all familiar with the act of weaving, you already know that threads are first strung on the loom in one direction. These are called the warp and are parallel to the selvages, the tightly woven edge of the fabric. Another thread is then woven through these threads, perpendicular to the first threads. These are called the weft.

Straight of grain refers to the length of the fabric, parallel to the selvages. Straight of grain has very little, if any, stretch. *Cross grain* refers to the width of the fabric, from selvage edge to selvage edge. There is quite a bit more stretch in this direction. *Bias* refers to a diagonal line through the weave. Any diagonal line is bias. *True bias* refers to the 45-degree angle through the weave. Bias is very stretchy. Cutting fabric on the bias leaves it very open to distortion by stretching, and just about anything can cause the fabric to stretch; heat from your iron and even just moving the fabric. There are times when we simply must cut on the bias and sew the seam on the bias. In those instances we just have to be extra careful.

19

OK, let's straighten the fabric. Fold your fabric in half lengthwise, selvage edge to selvage edge. Hold the fabric by the selvage edges and let the fabric hang freely from your hands. If there is a ripple in the fabric, slide one edge back and forth a little until the ripple disappears. The cut edge may no longer be lined up the way it was, but don't worry about that. It is important to align the selvage edges. Remember, the straight of grain is parallel to the selvage edges.

Straightening the fabric

Once you have made the selvage edges parallel, eliminating any ripples, lay the fabric on your cutting mat. I like to align the folded edge closest to me and right on the outer most grid line on my mat. I use the folded edge to align my ruler. The selvage edge is sometimes a little wavy and can cause inaccuracies in cutting.

Ideally, your cutting mat is on a surface that is about waist high and is accessible from all sides. If you don't have space on your kitchen counter, such as an island, you might purchase a utility worktable. Since the table is low,

you can raise the height by placing a length of pvc pipe from the hardware store over each of the legs, raising the surface as high as you need. The cross bar of the table legs will settle into the pipe. If the four lengths of pipe are the same, your table will be sturdy. The important thing is that you don't try to do a lot of rotary cutting at the height of a table, such as your dining room table, unless you are a very short person. It is way too hard on your back.

Looking at your 6" x 24" rotary cutting ruler, you will notice that there are markings in both directions: parallel to the cutting edge and perpendicular to the cutting edge. Align one of the lines perpendicular to the cutting edge exactly with the folded edge of your fabric. (If you don't align the markings with the fold exactly, you will find that upon opening your strip, you will have cut a V shaped strip instead of a straight strip.) The ruler should extend over the entire width of the folded fabric. The ruler will be on the fabric completely, not just covering the edge to be cut. In fact, the edge to be straightened will be cut away and is not covered by the ruler.

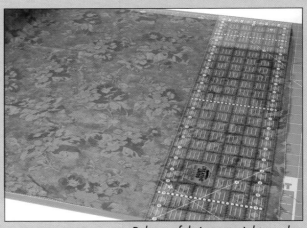
Ruler on fabric to straighten edge

You will be cutting with your dominant hand and securing the ruler with the other. Begin by walking around your table so that you are standing with the selvage edge in front of you. Place your hand on the ruler so that your fingers and thumb are away from the cutting edge and your little finger is behind the ruler on the cutting mat. Your little finger will help keep the ruler from shifting while you are cutting. The tips of your fingers should be no farther up the ruler than about the 8- or 9-inch mark. Start with the rotary cutter next to the lower corner of the ruler but behind the fabric. Roll the cutter forward, away from you, pressing through the fabric as you do. If your blade is new or newly sharpened, you should not have to press down too hard, but you do have to press down. About half way up the ruler, stop cutting. Without lifting the cutter, walk your other hand up the ruler and then continue to cut. Because your cutter is pressing against the ruler, you can cause a pivot point if your hand holding the ruler does not move forward along with the cutter. The mistake most often made is the ruler slipping, causing inaccurate cuts because the hand holding the ruler is way behind the

Rotary cutting

cutter, acting like a fulcrum. When you have finished the cut, retract the blade.

Remove the piece you cut without disturbing the newly cut edge and walk around the table so that now you are standing with the folded edge directly in front of you.

Now, let's say you want to cut a 3 1/2" strip as for the "4-Patch Strip" quilt project, directions beginning on page 106. Place your ruler so that it covers the newly cut edge. Align the 3 1/2" marking right on top of the newly cut edge. Part of your ruler will be on the mat, but the edge that you will cut against is on the fabric. The remainder of your fabric is to the right if you are right handed and to the left if you are left handed. With your cutter in your dominant hand and the other hand on the ruler as described previously, roll the cutter forward (always away from you) through the fabric until you're about half way up the ruler. Without lifting the cutter, walk your hand forward and continue cutting. When you've reached the other end, retract the blade.

Now, let's say you want to turn that 3 1/2" strip into 3 1/2" x 3 1/2" squares. Turn the strip on your mat a quarter rotation. Align one of the marks that are perpendicular to the cutting edge of the ruler with the cut edge of the strip. Remove the selvage edge just as you did when you straightened the fabric in the first place. Lay your ruler on the strip so that the 3 1/2" mark is aligned with the short edge you just cut and a perpendicular mark is aligned with a long edge of the strip. Use your rotary cutter to make the first cut. Remove the 3 1/2" x 3 1/2" square and repeat until you cut the entire strip into the number of squares you need. Cutting a strip into squares or rectangles is often referred to as *subcutting*. So, the directions in a pattern that tell you "subcut the 3 1/2" strip into 3 1/2" X 3 1/2" squares," would be telling you to do exactly as described above. Remember to retract the blade every time you put the cutter down.

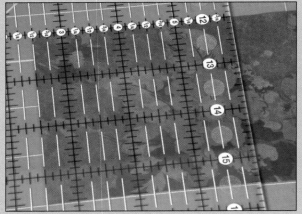
Ruler aligned for cutting squares

PIECING - by machine

Mary Ellen Hopkins, a well-known quilting teacher, designer and author, encourages quilters by telling them that they really don't need to sew with a strict 1/4" seam allowance. She suggests that whatever you do sew with, it should be consistent. She calls this a PPM - Personal Private Measurement. I happen to agree with her for the most part. Eventually you will expand beyond the very basics of quiltmaking and that's when you're going to want to perfect your 1/4" seam allowance. For the patterns in this book, a consistent seam allowance is more important. I always like to encourage my students to strive for good technique, such as the consistent 1/4" seam allowance, but allow themselves to enjoy the learning process. So if you can't seem to get the hang of the 1/4" seam allowance at first, then at least be consistent with whatever seam allowance you can achieve. Throughout this book, though, I will only be referring to the 1/4" seam allowance, and all of the comments regarding block sizes are assuming the 1/4" seam allowance. Eventually, I hope for you that you conquer the 1/4"seam allowance and that it becomes second nature to you.

You might like to test how well your machine is going to work with you on this 1/4" seam allowance issue. Use your rotary cutter and cut three pieces of scrap fabric into 1 1/2" x 3 1/2" rectangles. They can all even be from the same fabric. Sew two of the little strips together along the longest side with a 1/4" seam allowance, or at least what you think will be a 1/4"seam allowance. Press the seam allowances both in one direction without stretching or distorting your strips. In other words, press, don't iron.

Step to testing 1/4" seam allowance

Add the third strip to the unit you've just made so that the new seam is parallel to the first seam and again press the seam allowance to one side. Measure your square.

1/4"-presser feet

If your seam allowance is an accurate 1/4", and if you pressed and did not iron, you will find that your block will measure 3 1/2" x 3 1/2" square. Good for you! If your square is smaller than 3 1/2" x 3 1/2", I suggest that you sew your seams a thread's width LESS than 1/4". When you open the unit to press, the fabric is actually passing around the thread with which you sewed the seam. The thread can actually add to the width of the seam allowance. So when you read in a pattern that you are to sew with a scant 1/4" seam allowance, the directions are considering that the thread is part of the 1/4". Confused? Don't worry about it. Just be consistent.

As I mentioned previously, you will want to determine on the sewing bed of your machine where the 1/4" seam mark is. My machine has a tiny tick mark in the throat plate that I can use as a guide. Some machines will be fitted with a 1/4" foot. By guiding your fabric along the edge of the foot, you will be sewing a consistent 1/4"

seam allowance. And some presser feet are equipped with a built in "fence" on the side that represents the 1/4". By guiding the fabric against that fence you'll also be consistent. There are tools that are designed to be attached to the sewing machine sewing surface that are equipped with 1/4" guides as well as a number of other markings. And of course, you can place the masking tape or stack of sticky notes that I mentioned previously.

When sewing two patches of fabric together you will be stacking the two fabrics, right sides together. Now, I know you know this, but the "right side" is the side with the most vivid color, the prettier side. That is because a printed fabric only has dye put onto one side of the fabric. The "wrong side" then is the surface with no dye directly applied. Just to confuse things though, some fabrics are not printed but woven. In that case, both sides tend to look the same and are interchangeable. And just to confuse things even more, please note that there will be times when you will choose to use the wrong side as the right side. As I tell my students often, "You pay for both sides, you might as well use both sides!" So, when I say right sides together, I mean the side that you have chosen to be the right side, which, I am sure, will most often be the side with the print applied directly.

Guide the pair of patches so that the majority of the patch is to the left and front of the needle and the seam allowance will extend just 1/4" to the right of the needle. As you press the "accelerator," the feed dogs will move the fabric from the front of the needle to the back of the needle, all the while stitching.

Sewing patches

PRESSING VS IRONING

Before we begin piecing any blocks, I'd like to talk a little about pressing. It is important that you know the difference between pressing and ironing. When we press seam allowances during the piecing stage of our quiltmaking, we simply set the iron down and lift again. When we iron our shirts, we drag the iron back and forth over the surface of the garment to remove the wrinkles. So when I mention that you need to press the seam allowance to one direction or the other, I want you to bring the iron down onto your patch and lift it again. If you iron your block instead of pressing it, you run the risk of distorting your block. Distorted blocks often don't fit together with other blocks and your quilt top will not lie flat. And contrary to the popular myth, "it will quilt out," you cannot always correct problems with the quilting later.

Pressing is always done from the right side of your block. If you try to press from the wrong side, you will not be able to see what is happening to the seam and you run the risk of creating pleats and tucks. I begin by pressing

the seam just over the thread to set the stitches. Warming the fabric also makes it easier to press the patches open.

With my fingers I open the seam on the right side and press again. I lift the iron to move it to the next spot so that I don't stretch the fabric. Ironing stretches the fabric and stretching distorts. The distortion shows up as an arc.

Pressing from the right side

Remember; we press our seams, we iron our shirts.

Traditionally, quilters are told to press the seam allowances to the darker fabric. This makes sense *most of the time*. The seam allowances make a shadow behind a light fabric and can be seen from the right side of the quilt. By pressing to the darker fabric, the seam allowances are less likely to be seen. Now, that said, let me say that I don't believe you need to be held to the rule, pressing to the dark, in every instance. Sometimes you will have to press to the light because the block tells you that you have to. If I have a choice between pressing to a plain light fabric or a dark with an intersecting seam, I'm going to choose the light every time. Trying to press an intersecting seam just causes a bulky spot, which, by the way, can distort the block, too. So let the block guide you.

Using steam or not is another consideration. There are quilting teachers who tell their students to avoid steam. Adding steam to your pressing can cause the fabric to stretch. Adding steam and ironing instead of pressing will certainly cause you problems. I'll be honest; I do use steam. I think I get a better pressing. But remember, I'm pressing, not ironing. I recommend that you experiment some and see what works the best for you. Ultimately, your goal is to have a flat block that is consistent in size with all of the other blocks.

"SAMPLER"
56 1/2" x 56 1/2"
by Kathy Delaney, Overland Park, KS,
quilted by Kelly Ashton, 2004

26

CHAPTER 3
LET'S MAKE A QUILT

The most logical way I can think of to learn quiltmaking is by making a quilt! Following you will find 16 blocks that will teach a variety of techniques, beginning with the most basic block: a 4-Patch. From there you will learn more blocks, gradually becoming more complicated, until you have all 16 blocks. I recommend that you begin with the first block and build on your skills by making each of the blocks in order as they are presented.

Once you have the blocks finished, we'll finish the quilt. In this book are your private quilting lessons. Let me be the voice over your shoulder. I encourage you to take classes from your local quilt shops whenever possible. Join a guild if there is one in your area. Every time you meet another quilter, you are bound to learn something! Every teacher has her own way of doing things. The more you learn, the easier quiltmaking becomes. And by all means, have fun!

THE BLOCKS

Following are sixteen blocks for you to make while learning machine piecing techniques. When you complete these exercises you will have the basic skills needed for the projects in Chapter 6. In addition, you will have enough blocks to put together for a "Sampler" quilt. That is, a sampling of a variety of styles of blocks as well as techniques. And you will be on your way to completing your first quilt!

Fabric requirements:

• 11 fat quarters of coordinating prints for the blocks (Fabric is usually cut across the grain from selvage to selvage. So 1/4 yard is 9" x the width of the fabric. Four of these 9" strips equal a yard. A fat quarter begins with a yard of fabric cut into (2) 18" strips across the grain from selvage to selvage. Each of these strips is cut in half, resulting in a piece that is 18" x about 22".)

• 7/8 yard for sashing, the strips that separate the blocks
• 1/4 yard for corner stones, the small squares where the sashing strips intersect
• 1 3/4 yard for border, the frame to the design
• 1/2 yard for binding, the covering of the outside edges
• 3 1/2 yards for backing, sometimes called lining
• 62" x 62" batting, the filling between the top and the backing

(If you prefer, you may choose to use only four or five coordinating fabrics instead of the 11 fat quarters. Choose a fabric with at least three colors, preferably more, as your focus fabric. Then choose three or four fabrics that use the same colors in their prints, varying the size of the prints and even adding fabrics that will look like a solid even though they aren't really solid. In other words, you don't want all of the fabrics to have tiny little flowers or your quilt will not be very interesting. Make sure, too, that you have some very light and some very dark. You don't want all of your fabrics to be the same value. Purchase 1/2 yard of each of these and then continue down the list above.)

Each of the blocks will be 9" finished. This means that when you have completed the block, you will have a 9" block with 1/4" seam allowances. So, before it is sewn into your quilt top the block will measure 9 1/2" x 9 1/2". When you have completed all 16 blocks, I'll show you how to sash them, add a border and quilt and bind a 58" x 58" quilt to display on the wall of your sewing room. So, let's begin!

Piecing a 4-Patch Block

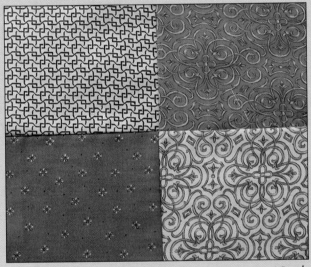

4-Patch

I think the easiest block to piece is the 4-Patch. This block is made up of four equal-sized squares and is an ideal way to begin because if your seam allowances miss that 1/4", you will still be able to make the block look as if it were pieced with precision. This block can be made any size and can be used in a lot of different ways, from the center of a Sawtooth Star to a border. And many of the techniques that you use to sew this block together are used everywhere else, as well.

Let us begin with four 5" squares. You can use four different fabrics or you may wish to only use two. My examples will show four: two dark fabrics and two lighter fabrics. My philosophy is "the more the merrier" when it comes to fabric!

First, lay out your four blocks on your sewing table next to your sewing machine so that the squares are in the arrangement you see in the photograph beginning these directions. Turn the upper right square over and place it on top of the upper left square. The right side of the right square will be on the inside, right sides together. (You will see this phrase often in your quilting career. Sometimes you will see it written RST.)

Sewing the squares together

Squares and one paired, ready for sewing.

With a 1/4" seam allowance, sew the two squares together. Without clipping your thread, sew the bottom two squares together the same way: lower-right square on top of lower-left square, right sides together. When sewing two patches together with a short straight seam, I don't usually pin the two pieces together. If it will make you feel more secure, pin away!

Without clipping the two units apart, press the seam allowance to the darker of the two squares on both units. Notice that they will each be pressed in opposite directions.

Bring the top unit down over the bottom unit, right sides together, and align the center seam allowances. Because the seam allowances are pressed in opposite directions you will find that they snug up to each other tightly.

Aligning the seam allowances between fingers

There are several ways to pin the two units together in the center. Each quilter will have her favorite way. Quilter A will place a pin straight down into the two seam allowances to get them aligned. Then she will place another pin in front of the seam allowances and one just behind, perpendicular to the raw edge, making sure that the seam allowances don't shift. Finally she removes the first pin and sews the seam.

Pinning with 2 pins

Quilter B will follow the same method as described above, but the pin just in front of the seam allowance and the pin just behind are put on an angle instead of perpendicular to the raw edge. Some quilters feel that the pins on an angle keep the fabric from shifting better.

Quilter C will place her pins parallel and 1/4" from the raw edges on the patches being sewn. As the machine approaches the pin it is removed.

When I pin the seam allowances, I snug the seam allowances into each other tightly and place one pin just in front of the seam allowances so that nothing

shifts. Eventually you will find the method that suits you the best.

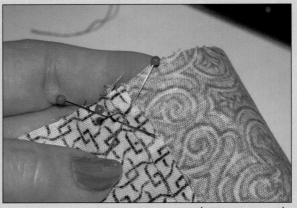

Pinning with 2 pins on angle

Pinning parallel to the raw edge

The way I pin

Before pressing the seam allowance, turn the block over and notice that the pressed seam allowances are in opposite directions. You are going to press the new seam in opposite directions, splitting the seam in the center at the intersection. To do this, you will first have to clip the thread that connected the two units in the first place and then release a stitch or two in the center of the previous seam. Most of the time you can do this by holding the two halves of the seam just on either side of the intersection and giving it a twist. If that little twist will not break the stitch, then use your scissors and clip the first stitch or two.

Twisting the center to release stitch

Now lay the block on your ironing board and, with your fingers, press the seam allowances so that they are all going in the same direction around the center. At the center intersection you will find a tiny replica of the 4-Patch. When you turn the block over and press with the iron, you should notice that the center of your block lies very flat, with no bulkiness. (Never press from the back of the block with the iron. You are very likely to press in a pleat on the seam.) And remember, press,

don't iron. Ironing is for shirts. Ironing will distort your block.

Wrong side of block after pressing

If you have been very careful with your piecing and pressing, your block will be 9 1/2" square. To be sure, place your 12 1/2" square ruler on your block. The 4 3/4" marks, both horizontal and vertical, will be directly over the center seams. Use your rotary cutter to trim any excess fabric that is peaking out from under your square ruler on the right and top edges (if you are left handed, trim the left side and top). Rotate the block 180 degrees and repeat.

Beginning on page 104 you will find directions for a quilt project that uses 4-Patch blocks.

Piecing a Rail Fence Block

Traditionally, a Rail Fence Block is created with three fabrics; a light, a medium and a dark. And notice that ultimately this is a 4-Patch block as you made beginning on page 28. The only difference is we're going to piece each of the four patches before putting them all together. The method we're going to use is called strip piecing. That is, we will begin with strips of fabric that we sew together into a strip set, a set of strips sewn together, and then cut the strip set into units that we'll sew together with other units.

Three strips ready for sewing

Rail Fence block

From each of your three fabrics, cut a 2" x about 22" strip as described beginning on page 19. The easiest way to sew the blocks is to begin by sewing your strips into a strip set. In other words, we are going to sew all the strips together and then cut the set into blocks.

Decide what order you would like to sew your strips and sew two of the strips, right sides together, with a 1/4" seam allowance. My example shows the strips from light to dark. Consider that if you place the light between the medium and dark or the dark between the light and medium you might lose the pattern that these blocks traditionally make.

Press the seam allowance to one side and sew the third strip to the first two, placing the third strip, right sides together over the second strip. Press the seam allowance in the same direction as you did the first. Be sure to press, don't iron, so that you won't cause the strip set to "frown," or stretch into a curve instead of remaining straight.

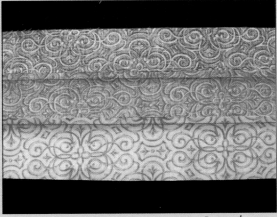

Pressed seams

Some quilters believe that by sewing one pair of strips together in one direction and then adding the third, sewing in the opposite direction, you can avoid creating an arc with your strip set. I think you can sew the strips in opposite directions if all of the strips are the same length. When the strips are different lengths, I think there is waste and a chance that I will run short.

Some quilters believe that sewing all of the pairs in the same direction is crucial. I have to say, I think that the pressing is the most important step to ensure that the strip set is straight.

If you are very careful in your pressing (no ironing!), you will end up with a straight strip set. (You may wish to review pressing, beginning on page 24.) If you succumb to the temptation to iron the seam allowances, you will find that your strip set frowns and is no longer straight. Your blocks will not be square.

Pressing across ironing board instead of the length

I have been known to suggest to my students that they press a strip set in sections by laying the strip set across the ironing board vertically instead of horizontally. By doing so, it's almost impossible to iron and the strip set is less likely to frown. Find the method that works best

for you. Just remember, press, don't iron.

If you sewed your strips with a 1/4" seam allowance, your strip set will measure 5" wide. With your 12 1/2" square ruler or your 6" x 24" ruler, you will be able to cut your blocks. Unless you removed the selvages before you began sewing the strips together (I never do) you will have to remove them now. If you did remove the selvages, you still need to straighten the end.

Begin by laying your strip set horizontally on your rotary cutting mat. If you are right handed, the straightened end of the set will be to your left. If you are left handed, the straightened end of the set will be on your right. Place your 12 1/2" square ruler so that the left cutting edge is to the right of the left selvage edge, about 1/2" from the edge of the fabric. (If you are left handed, just do the opposite.) Align a horizontal line on your ruler so that it is lined up on one of your seams. One and a half inches away should be a line on the ruler, again, lined up with the other seam. Walk around to the other side of the mat and, with your rotary cutter, remove the selvages. If you are working

Ruler on strip set

on a counter that won't allow you to go to the other side, rotate the mat without disturbing the fabric and ruler.

Go back to the other side of your mat again and place the cutting edge of the ruler 5 inches away from the edge you just cut. The 5" mark will be right over the cut edge and two of the perpendicular lines on the ruler will be right over the seams. Cut the block from the strip set. For a Rail Fence block you will need to cut four.

Wrong side showing seams pressed

Take a look at the picture of the block at the beginning of these directions. Notice that the upper left and the lower right squares are vertical and the upper right and lower left blocks are horizontal. Lay your four blocks on your sewing table near your sewing machine so that they look like the picture. With 1/4" seam allowances, and right sides together, sew the top two squares together and sew the bottom two squares together just as you did when you made the 4-Patch block described previously without clipping the threads between units. In both

cases, press the seam allowances toward the vertical block.

Bring the top unit down over the bottom unit, right sides together. Because the two units are still connected, there is only one way to do it. Line up the center seam. The seam allowances will be pressed in opposite directions and you will be able to snug them together. Pin the center intersection with the method you prefer. However, pinning right on the seams can shift them and defeat the purpose. Sew the two halves together with a 1/4" seam allowance.

Remember that little trick you did with the 4-Patch block to press the two halves of the seam in opposite directions? Do it again on this block and your center will be flat. Your block should measure 9 1/2"x 9 1/2".

Beginning on page 128 you will find directions for a quilt project that uses Rail Fence blocks.

Piecing a 9-Patch Block

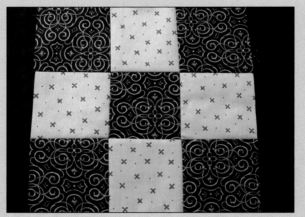
9-Patch block

Three rows of three squares each make the 9-Patch Block. By pressing the seams in opposite directions, the patches fit together snuggly and the block lies flat. Often you will see this block with two contrasting fabrics, but you can use as many as nine different fabrics, 5 darks and 4 lights. (Or 5 lights and 4 darks.) My example uses two fabrics.

Three units strung together

9 squares laid out ready to sew

With your rotary cutter and rotary ruler, cut the nine 3 1/2" squares just as you did when you made your 4-Patch block, beginning on page 28.

Lay your squares out on the table near your sewing machine so that they look like the photograph of the finished block. Now, separate the squares into 3 rows. Place the second square on top of the left square, right sides together, and sew with a 1/4" seam. Without cutting your thread, repeat with the first and second blocks of the second row and then again with the third. You should have three units all strung together.

Seam allowances pressed in opposite directions

Without clipping the units apart, press the seams to one side. In each case, press the seams to the darker fabric. Notice that in doing so, you will alternate the direction of the seams.

Now you can add the third square to each of the rows as you did the second squares. Place the third square over the second square, right sides together, and sew with a 1/4" seam allow-ance. Do not clip the threads between the rows. Press the seam allowances toward the darker fabric, again alternating the directions. Now you will have three rows all strung together.

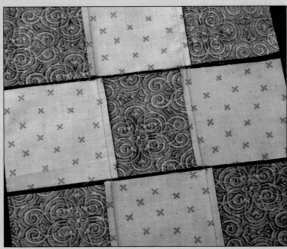

Three rows pressed

Wrong side of block showing the seam allowances

Bring row one down over row two, right sides together, and pin the intersections as you did in the previous blocks. Because the rows are connected by thread, you won't be able to make a mistake in the sequence. Add the third row to the second in the same manner. Again, because the rows are connected by thread, you won't be able to make a mistake.

Before pressing the last two seam allowances, turn your block over and notice the previous seam allowances. Usually your block will tell you which way the seams want to go. They will always take the route of least resistance. In other words, your block will not want you to press the seam allowances against an intersecting seam allowance. It causes bulk. If you pressed your seam allowances as my directions indicate, then you have pressed the seam allowances toward the center. The seam allowances for the rows will be pressed away from the center.

Remember, you are pressing, not ironing! Your block should measure 9 1/2" x 9 1/2".

The gallery will show you some ideas for quilts with the 9-Patch block.

Piecing a Variable 9-Patch Block

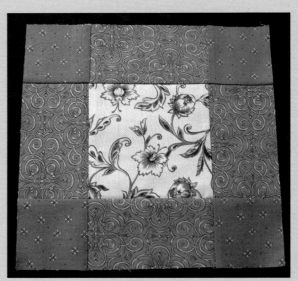

Variable 9-Patch Block

This block is an excellent choice if you have a special fabric you would like to highlight. The block is made with nine pieces, just as the 9-Patch block; however, the center square is larger than the rest. Making the center larger means that the blocks directly adjacent must be larger, which makes them rectangles.

Begin by choosing three fabrics; the center focus, and two contrasting but coordinating fabrics.

With your rotary cutter and your rotary cutting ruler, cut a 5" x 5" square from your focus fabric, the fabric you chose with several colors in the print. In a future quilt this square could be a toile (a scene depicting people or animals) or a floral cluster or Santa Claus, whatever you like. Center the corner of your 12 1/2" square ruler over the portion of the design you'd like to highlight. Cut the side and top. (For a refresher on how to rotary cut, please see page 19.) Turn the piece of fabric 180 degrees and place the ruler over the piece you just cut so that the 5" lines, both horizontal and vertical, are on the edges you just cut. Repeat your cuts on the side and top.

Second cut for the 5" square

From the fabric you've chosen for the four corners, cut four 2 3/4" squares. And from your third fabric, cut four 2 3/4" x 5" rectangles.

Lay the pieces on the table near your sewing machine so that they look like the picture of the Variable 9-Patch block pictured at the beginning of these directions. Sew the block together in rows just as you did the 9-Patch block. For a refresher, see page 35. Your pressing will be the same as for the 9-Patch block as well. Your block should measure 9 1/2" x 9 1/2".

Piecing a Half-Square Triangle Block

1/2-square triangle

This block is a square that is divided in half to make two right angle triangles. It is a very basic block and works very well as an element in a number of other block designs. There are several different methods for making this block, from using a template to create the two halves to quick methods using the rotary cutter. There are even several methods for making multiples of this unit. I'm

37

going to give you two of my favorite quick methods.

A basic formula for making any size 1/2-square triangle unit is to measure the straight side of one of the triangles and add 7/8"; 1/2" is for total seam allowance and 3/8" is for the diagonal seam allowance. So a 9" finished block begins with a 9 7/8" square. I will always round up to 10" and after sewing I will use my square ruler to trim it to the right size. This way I am assured of a perfectly square block.

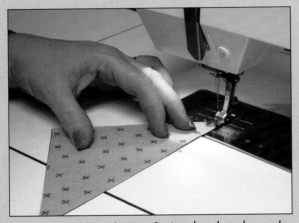
Sewing 2 triangles along long edge

One method for making our 9 1/2" x 9 1/2" half-square triangle block is to begin with a 10" square of two fabrics, a light and dark for contrast. With your rotary cutter, cut both squares in half, diagonally. Match a light square with a dark square and sew a 1/4" seam allowance along the longest edge. The problem with this method is that you are sewing along the bias edge. The bias edge is the least stable and will very likely stretch as you are sewing.

Another method is to begin with a 9 1/2" square of two fabrics, a light and dark for contrast. With a ruler and pencil, draw a line diagonally across the wrong side of the lighter fabric. With right sides together, align the two squares, matching the raw edges. Sew a seam right on the line that you drew. With a rotary cutter, make a cut 1/4" from the sewn line. Save the two small triangles you've cut for another project or discard.

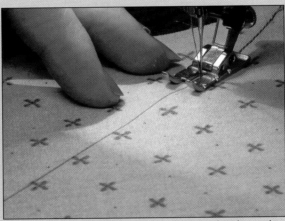
Sew on the drawn line

Cut 1/4" away from seam

With your iron, set the seam and then press the seam to the darker fabric. Remember, press, don't iron. You should have a 9 1/2" x 9 1/2" square.

Yet another method makes two units at once. (This is my favorite method.) Begin with a 10" square of two fabrics, a light and a dark for contrast. With a ruler and a pencil, draw a line diagonally across the wrong side of the lighter square. Lay the two squares, right sides together, matching the outside edges. Sew 1/4" from the line on both sides of the line. With your rotary cutter or scissors, cut on the line. Press the seams to the darker fabric. With your square ruler, trim the blocks to 9 1/2" x 9 1/2", making sure that the diagonal line of the ruler lines up exactly with the diagonal seam.

To make a large number of 1/2-square triangle units, there are commercial paper grids that guide you in sewing and cutting with very little effort. Refer to the directions for the "Birds in the Air" quilt, beginning on page 114, for directions using these products.

Cut on the line

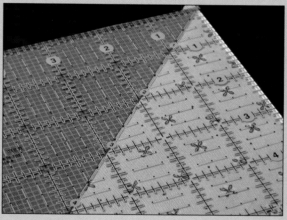

Align the seam and the diagonal marking

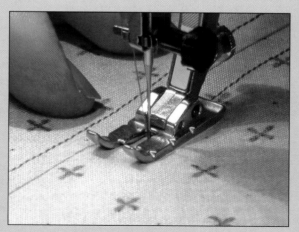

Sew 1/4" from both sides of line

Piecing a Quarter-Square Triangle Block (Hour Glass)

We're going to use some of the same easy techniques for the Hour Glass that we used for the 1/2-Square Triangle. My favorite method will yield two blocks at once. And, again, we'll be making a 9" finished block.

Begin with two 10 1/2" squares from two fabrics, a light and a dark for contrast. Draw a line diagonally across the

1/4-square triangle

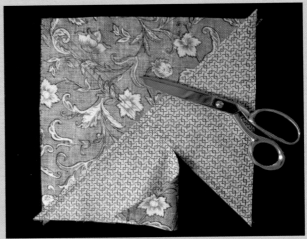

Cut on the line

back of the lighter fabric as you did for the 1/2-square triangle. Sew 1/4" from the line on both sides and then cut the two halves apart, just as you did previously. Press the seam to the darker fabric.

Now, place the two blocks, right sides together, rotating one of the blocks so that the seam allowances are pressed in opposite directions. Remember the 4-Patch? Same principle. The center seams will snug together. If you wish, you may place a pin or three to secure the two blocks.

With your ruler, draw a line diagonally across the back of one of the blocks, crossing the seam. Sew 1/4" from the line on both sides and then cut the two halves apart, just as you did previously.

Remember pressing the second seam on the 4-Patch?

Remember how you split the seam and pressed the two halves in opposite directions so that all the seams were pressed in the same direction around the center? Do the

same thing for the Hour Glass block. You will have two identical blocks. With your rotary cutter, trim one of the blocks, centering the crossed seams, so that it is 9 1/2" x 9 1/2" square. Save the second Hour Glass block for another block in your quilt. You will use it later.

As for the 1/4-square triangle blocks, there are commercial paper grids that guide your sewing multiple 1/4-square triangle blocks. Someone at your quilting supply store will be able to show you the different products.

Piecing a Flying Geese Block

There are so many really neat ways to make this block that it's hard for me to limit the directions to just one basic method here. Depending on the ultimate purpose, you might use a different method each time. Throughout this

Sampler quilt you will find this block being used several times. Each time you use the block, I'll give you another way to make it.

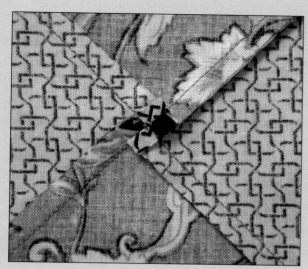

The back of finished 1/4-square triangle block

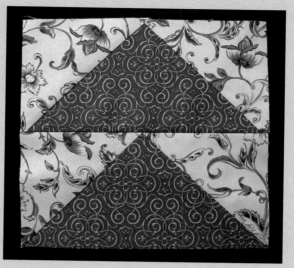

Flying geese block

For the most basic method, you will need a 10 1/4" x 10 1/4" square of one fabric and two 5 3/8" x 5 3/8" squares of another fabric.

With your rotary cutter and rotary ruler, cut the larger square in half diagonally in both directions so that you have four 1/4-square triangles. You will need two of them. Set the other two aside for another project. Cut the two smaller squares in half diagonally. You will need all four of these 1/2-square triangles. The large triangles are our "geese" and the smaller triangles are our "sky."

With right sides together, align the longest edge of the smaller triangle, the bias edge, with one of the short edges of the large triangle, also a bias edge. The adjacent straight edges will also perfectly match. The smaller triangle will extend past the top of the larger triangle.

The trick to sewing this seam is to guide the fabric through the machine without actually holding on to it. If you hold it, you will stretch it. You just want to gently guide it. When you have sewn the seam with a 1/4" seam allowance, very carefully press the seam allowance to the smaller triangle.

Repeat this step with the second small triangle. Align the longest edge, the bias edge, with the other bias edge of the larger triangle. Again, the straight edges line up perfectly. The end of the smaller triangle will extend past the top of the larger triangle. When you begin sewing your 1/4" seam allowance, the needle will begin the stitch right in the V where the tips cross.

Again, just guide the fabric through the machine without actually holding it. When you have pressed the seam allowance to the second small triangle, trim all of the little

Pieces laid out and matched for sewing

This is one of those instances. Press the seam allowance to the top unit. Your block will measure 9 1/2" x 9 1/2".

Pieces lined up for stitching showing the needle in the V

"ears" sticking out from behind the block. It will measure 5" x 9 1/2". You will be making two of these flying geese units.

Set the two halves of the block on the table near your sewing machine so that they look like the block example at the beginning of these directions. Flip the bottom unit up onto the top unit, with right sides together. With a 1/4" seam allowance, sew the two units together. As you approach the center, make sure that you stitch right through the X created by the previous two seams or a thread's width to the right of the X. Sewing to the left of the X will cut the very tip of the triangle off and you don't want to do that.

Remember when I mentioned that sometimes the block would tell you which way to press the seam allowance?

Sewing through the X

Wrong side showing pressed seam

COMBINING WHAT WE'VE LEARNED

Double 4-Patch

Double 4-Patch

A Double 4-Patch is a 4-Patch block made with two smaller 4-Patch units and two squares the same size as the unit. Begin by cutting two squares 5" x 5". Use a different fab-

ric than the ones you'll use in the smaller 4-Patch units.

Choosing two more fabrics, cut four 2 3/4" x 2 3/4" squares from each. Using the same techniques that you used in making the 4-Patch, beginning on page 28, construct two identical 4-Patch units that will measure 5" x 5" when complete.

All the pieces that make the block.

Lay the two 4-Patch units and the two 5" squares out on your sewing table near your machine so that they look like the picture. Using the same techniques, treating the 4-Patch units the same as your squares, construct the Double 4-Patch. When pressing, press the seams to the squares, whether they are dark or not. The block will measure 9 1/2" x 9 1/2".

Double 9-Patch

This time, instead of five squares of one fabric and four

squares of another, you will need five 9-Patch blocks that measure 3 1/2" x 3 1/2", and four squares that measure 3 1/2" x 3 1/2".

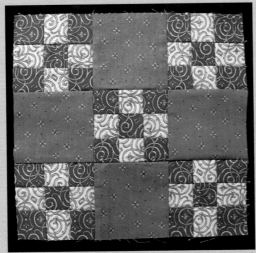

Double 9-Patch

There's a pretty nifty way to strip piece a 9-Patch that works great when you need to make more than one! Begin by choosing two fabrics for the 9-Patch blocks. You will need to cut three strips of one and three strips of the other. With your rotary cutter and ruler, cut each of the six strips 1 1/2" x 18".

Arrange the strips into two sets, as you did when you made the Rail Fence block beginning on page 32. This time you will pair two of one fabric with one of the other, alternating the fabrics. Notice in the picture I have labeled the strip sets "A" and "B" for reference as I complete the directions.

Be sure to sew with a consistent 1/4" seam allowance so that your strip sets will measure 3 1/2" x 18" when you are finished pressing. Press all of the seams to the darker of the two fabrics. Notice that between the two strip sets

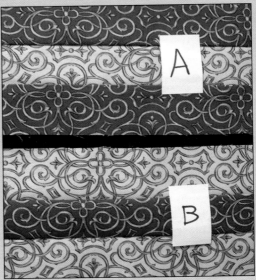

Strips sets A and B

the seam allowances will be pressed in opposite directions.

With your rotary cutter, straighten one of the ends of each of the strip sets and then from strip set "A" cut ten 1 1/2" x 3 1/2" units. From strip set "B" cut five 1 1/2" x 3 1/2" units.

On your sewing table near your machine, arrange the units so that they look like the photograph. Notice that because you pressed all of the seam allowances to one fabric, the seams oppose and snug into each other at the intersections. Pin as described on page 30 and sew with a 1/4" seam allowance. The little 9-Patch blocks will measure 3 1/2" x 3 1/2".

On your sewing table near your machine, arrange the little 9-Patch blocks and the 3 1/2" x 3 1/2" squares into a 9-Patch design. With a 1/4" seam allowance, sew the block together in the same manner you did when you

Parts of small 9-Patch

From each of the two fabrics rotary cut two 6" squares. On the wrong side of the two lighter fabrics, draw a diagonal line from one corner to the opposite corner. With right sides together, pair a light square with a dark square and sew 1/4" from the line on both sides of the line. Repeat with the second pair of squares. Review making the 1/2-square triangle unit on page 37.

With your sewing shears or rotary cutter, cut through the sewn squares on the line that you drew. Press the seam allowances to the darker of the two fabrics. With your rotary cutter and 12 1/2-inch square ruler, trim the blocks so that they each measure 5" square.

Arrange the 1/2-square triangle units on your sewing table near your sewing machine so that they look like the picture of the block shown below.

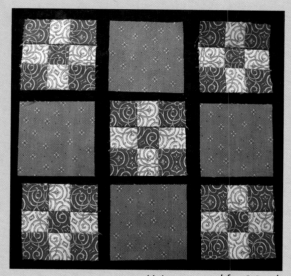

Units arranged for 9-Patch

Windmill block.

made your first 9-Patch block as described on page 35. After pressing, your Double 9-Patch will measure 9 1/2" x 9 1/2".

Windmill

A Windmill block is a 4-Patch made from four identical 1/2-square triangle units, rotated around the center point. Begin by choosing two fabrics with contrast.

When you align the blocks, right sides together for sewing, you should notice that the diagonal seams snug together because the seam allowances are pressed in opposite directions. It is important that when you sew your seam allowance you maintain a very consistent 1/4". In this case, your consistency will assure you that all your points will be meeting in the center of the block without being cut off. Sew the four blocks together just as you did when you made your first 4-Patch block beginning on page 28.

Press the seam allowances so that they are pressed in the same direction as the bias seams are pressed. Align the two new units, being sure to match the seam allowances in the middle. I suggest that you use the method you like the best and pin the center intersection. When I match the center, I do place a pin straight through where the new seam intersects with the diagonal seams on one unit and then through the same place on the second unit. While this pin is in place I pin just to the left of center and remove the first pin. Sew with a 1/4" seam allowance.

Remember that twist you do in the center of every 4-Patch? Do it again and press the seam allowances all in the same direction as the previous seam allowances. On the wrong side of your block you should have a tiny replica of your Pinwheel block. On the right side of your block, the center will lie flat and your points will all come together in the center. Your block should measure 9 1/2" x 9 1/2".

Remember, pressing is important. Ironing will pull your blocks out of square and the whole block will

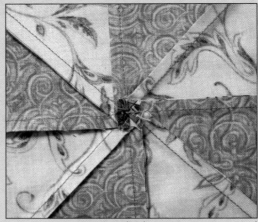

Wrong side showing seams pressed

be distorted. Any distortion could cause the points to be cut off when the blocks are joined.

Combining a Quarter - Square and a Variable 9-Patch

This block is going to combine the Hour Glass block and the Variable 9-Patch for a variation on the block you made before. Instead of the focus fabric in the center, you'll use the second Hour Glass block that you set aside earlier. (See page 40.)

Choose two fabrics that are not in the Hour Glass block. From one of the fabrics, cut four 2 3/4" x 2 3/4" squares. From the other fabric cut four 2 3/4" x 5" rectangles. Trim the Hour Glass block so that it is 5" x 5", making sure that the center crossed seams are exactly in the center. The 2 1/2" marks, both horizontally and vertically will center on the intersection of the two diagonal seams.

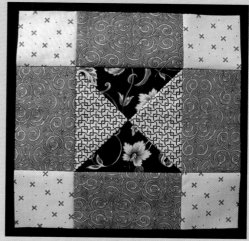

Variable 9-Patch with Hour Glass Center

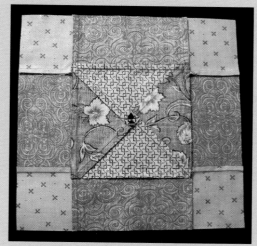

Wrong side of the finished block

Arrange the squares and rectangles on your table near your sewing machine and construct this block in the same way that you did your first Variable 9-Patch. This time, however, when pressing your seams, press them all to the rectangle whether it is the darker fabric or not. This way the seams will snug when combining units and the block will lie flat. When you sew the rows together, press the seams away from the center. Your block will measure 9 1/2" x 9 1/2".

Hourglass Pinwheel

By combining four identical Hour Glass units and rotating them around the center point, you can create another variation of the Pinwheel block.

Begin by choosing two fabrics, a light and a dark or a print and a solid for contrast. From each of the two fabrics cut two 5 3/4" x 5 3/4" squares.

Using the same techniques you used to make the Hour Glass block, beginning on page 40, make four Hour Glass units. Trim the units so that they each measure 5" x 5". You especially want to remove the little "ears" that are extending past the edges.

On your sewing table near your sewing machine, lay out the four units so that they look like the picture of the Hour Glass Pinwheel pictured below.

Trimming the Hour Glass block

Pinwheel made with four Hour Glass blocks

Alternating the direction of the blocks creates this design. Unfortunately, it also eliminates the opposing seam allowances. Very carefully, pin the two corners so that the seam allowances won't shift. You don't want to lose your points that are created by the triangles. Sew with a consistent 1/4" seam allowance.

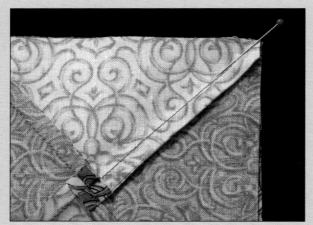

Blocks pinned

Press the seam allowances to the darker fabric. Depending on the fabric you are using, you may find it better to press the seams open to eliminate the bulk, or at least distribute it evenly. A bulkier fabric will ask

that you press the seams open. If you must, go ahead. Ultimately, your quilt is stronger by pressing the seams to one side. But there will be times that you must press the seams open.

When you sew the two halves of the block together, you will want to carefully match the center seams as well as the diagonal seams in the corner. While the center seams are pressed in opposite directions, the corner seams aren't. Very carefully pin the intersections so the seam allowances won't shift. Sew with a consistent 1/4" seam allowance. At the center be very careful to sew through the crossed threads or a thread's width to the right of the crossed threads so as not to cut off any of your points.

Press the final seam open to distribute the bulk in the center of the block.

Seams pressed open

The Hour Glass Table Runner project, beginning on page 108, uses this block.

Wrong side of block showing pressed seams

Churn Dash

Combining 1/2-square triangle units and two strips of the Rail Fence makes the Churn Dash block, sometimes called Greek Square, Monkey Wrench or Double Monkey Wrench. Choose two fabrics with contrast for this block.

Churn Dash

One will be considered background to the design. From each of the fabrics, cut two 4" x 4" squares. With right sides together, pair two of the contrasting squares and mark a diagonal line on the wrong side of the lighter fabric, just as you have each time you've sewn a 1/2-square triangle unit. Sew 1/4" from the line on both sides of the line just as you have before. Repeat with a second pair of squares. With scissors or a rotary cutter, cut on the line that you drew and press the seams to the darker fabric. Trim the four blocks so that they measure 3 1/2" x 3 1/2".

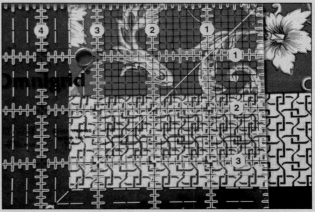

Cutting the strip set into blocks

From each of the same two fabrics you chose for the 1/2-square triangle units, cut one 2" x 16" strip. As you did when you made the Rail Fence block, sew the strips together with a 1/4" seam allowance. Press the seam allowance to the darker fabric, being careful not to stretch the strips, causing a frown. The strip set should measure 3 1/2" wide.

With your rotary cutter and rotary ruler, straighten one end of the strip set and cut (4) 3 1/2" x 3 1/2" squares.

Now you need to decide if your design is from the lighter or the darker fabric. Either way is fine. It is totally up to you. The fabric you did not choose for the design is the background. From the background fabric, cut a 3 1/2" x 3 1/2" square.

Wrong side of block showing seams pressed

On your sewing table near your sewing machine, arrange the squares so that they look like the photograph of the block at the beginning of these directions. Construct the block as you have all of the 9-Patch blocks you have made. Press the seams that combine the 1/2-square triangle units and the strip set units toward the 1/2-square triangle units. Press the seams that combine the strip set units and the center square to the center square. Press the seams that join the rows away from the center row. I know I have always said to press toward the least resistance. If your fabric really wants to be pressed toward the center, it will tell you. Listen to it. Either way, press, don't iron! The block will measure 9 1/2" x 9 1/2".

Dutchman's Puzzle

The Dutchman's Puzzle block combines four identical Flying Geese blocks in a 4-Patch block. You will need a total of eight Flying Geese units, which means a lot of bias edges! But there is a really slick way to make four units at a time. Begin with two contrasting fabrics. Decide which will be the geese and which will be the sky. From the geese fabric, cut two 5 3/4" x 5 3/4" squares. From the sky fabric, cut (8) 3 1/8" x 3 1/8" squares.

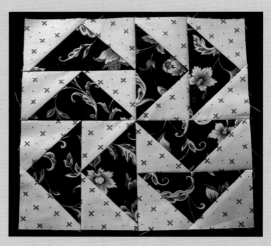
Dutchman's Puzzle block

With right sides together, align a small square onto one corner of a large square. Align a second square onto the opposite corner, diagonally from the first small square. The two small squares will overlap a little in the center. With a pencil and ruler, draw a line diagonally through the center of both of the small squares. Sew 1/4" from the drawn line, on both sides of the line.

Small squares on the large and the drawn line and sewn

With scissors or a rotary cutter, cut on the line that you drew. Press, don't iron, the small triangles open. The seams will be pressed to the small triangles. You now have a large triangle with two small triangles attached. It resembles a heart shape.

First half of flying geese unit

Align a small square on the free corner of the large triangle on or at the bottom of the heart shape. One corner of the small square will extend past the point where the two small triangles are joined. Draw a line diagonally

through the small square right through the center of the heart shape. Sew 1/4" from the drawn line on both sides of the line.

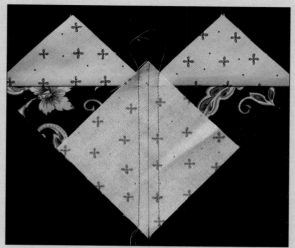

Drawn line and the sewn seams

With scissors or a rotary cutter, cut on the line that you drew. Press the small triangles open. The seams will be pressed to the small triangle. You have four flying geese units that measure 2 3/4" x 5". Sew two units together to create a 5" x 5" unit just as you did beginning on page 41. Sew the other two units together to create a second 5" x 5" unit.

Repeat all of the described steps, using the second large square and the second set of four small squares. You will have a total of four 5" x 5" Flying Geese units.

Arrange the four blocks on your sewing table near your sewing machine so that they look like the photograph of the Dutchman's Puzzle block at the beginning of these directions. Using the same techniques you have used for all of the 4-Patch blocks that you have made, sew the four units together. Because there are so many seams coming together in the center, you might consider sewing from the center out in each direction. This will secure the center and it will allow you to see the crossing threads on both sides as you sew through the points.

Unit cut apart and one unit pressed

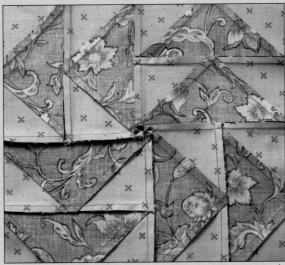
Pressed seams on wrong side

The block will tell you which direction to press the seam allowance. It is not to an intersecting seam! Your block will measure 9 1/2" x 9 1/2".

Ohio Star

The Ohio Star is a 9-Patch block combining Hour Glass units with squares. Choose two fabrics that contrast. One is the star and one is the background. You might choose a print for the background and a solid for the star or the other way around. Refer to page 39 to review constructing the Hour Glass unit.

Ohio Star

Begin by cutting two 4 1/4" x 4 1/4" squares from each of the two fabrics. Pair the squares and draw a line diagonally from corner to corner on the back of the lighter of the two squares. Sew 1/4" from the line on both sides of the line. With scissors or rotary cutter, cut on the drawn line and press the seam allowance to the darker fabric.

Repeat with the second pair. Align a pair of the 1/2-square triangle units so that the seam allowances snug in opposite directions. Draw a line through the center of one of the squares on the wrong side, crossing the seam. Sew 1/4" from the drawn line on both sides of the line. With scissors or a rotary cutter, cut on the drawn line. Using your twist trick, press the seam allowances all in the same direction around the center. Repeat with the second pair. Trim the four Hour Glass units to 3 1/2" x 3 1/2", making sure that the intersecting seams are exactly in the center.

Version A

Decide whether you want a dark star on a light background or vice versa. I suggest that you arrange the Hour Glass units on a piece of one of the fabrics so that they look like the photograph of the Ohio Star block. Do you like it? Now arrange the Hour Glass units on the other fabric in the same way. Changes the look of the star,

doesn't it? Which one do you like better? Cut four 3 1/2" x 3 1/2" squares of that one and one 3 1/2" x 3 1/2" square of the other for the center. On your sewing table

Version B

near your sewing machine, arrange the squares so that they look like the photograph of the Ohio Star block. Using the same techniques with which you are familiar from sewing all of the other 9-Patch blocks, sew the

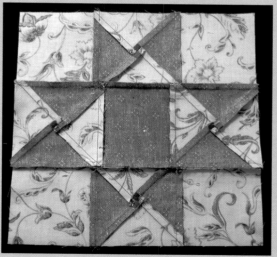

Ohio Star showing the seam allowances on the wrong side

squares together into rows and then the rows into the block. Your block should measure 9 1/2" x 9 1/2". Press all your seams to the squares, not the Hour Glass blocks. Press the rows to the center.

Sawtooth Star

Sawtooth Star block

The Sawtooth Star is made with four Flying Geese units and five squares. It is another good opportunity to use your focus fabric, as the center of the star is the same size as the center of the Variable 9-Patch you made on page 36. In fact, this block is a Variable 9-Patch with Flying Geese units where we previously had rectangles!

Here is yet another method for creating a Flying Geese unit. Begin by choosing two fabrics that contrast. This time the Geese are the background and the sky is the points of the star. With your rotary cutter cut (4) 2 3/4" x 5" rectangles and (4) 2 3/4" x 2 3/4" squares from the background fabric. From the star fabric, cut a 5" x 5" square

for the star center and (8) 2 3/4" x 2 3/4" squares for the star points.

With right sides together, place a star point square on a background rectangle, aligning the outside edges. With a pencil and a ruler, draw a line diagonally across the square so that it extends from the center of the rectangle to the outside corner. Sew on the line. Press the triangle you have created to the outside corner.

Notice that the corner now has three layers of fabric. You may be tempted to remove the bottom two layers, but don't do it! Let's say that your squares slipped a little and, in addition, you distorted the triangle in your pressing. If you leave the bottom layer, the original rectangle, your final sewing can be using the rectangle as your guide and you keep the accuracy. Instead, just remove the center layer, the other half of the small square, with your scissors, leaving no more than a 1/4" seam allowance.

Steps to sewing the square to the rectangle.

Now, repeat with a second square, placing it on the opposite end of the rectangle, right sides together. With a pencil and ruler, draw a line diagonally across the square so that it extends from the center of the rectangle to the outside corner. Sew on the drawn line. Press the triangle to the outside corner. Again, remove just the center layer of fabric, keeping the original rectangle intact. If your triangles are very distorted, you may trim them to match the rectangle.

From the other three rectangles and the remaining six squares, make three more Flying Geese units. Mary Ellen Hopkins developed this method of making your Flying Geese units and she calls them connectors. Remember? Mary Ellen Hopkins is the one who developed the concept of the PPM - personal private measurement. She acknowledges that this method makes parts of your quilt a little bulkier with two layers of fabric. However, if you machine quilt it won't matter. And if you hand quilt, you can avoid quilting inside those triangles. The point is, you are more likely to be accurate!

On your sewing table near your sewing machine, arrange the squares and rectangles so that they look like the photograph of the Sawtooth Star at the beginning of these directions. Sew the block together just as you have every other Variable 9-Patch. Press the seams to the squares in each row. Press the seams that join the rows away from the center. Your block should measure 9 1/2" x 9 1/2".

Congratulations! You have completed all of your blocks for your sampler quilt! You will find directions for the next step, which is to make your blocks into a finished quilt, in Chapter 5 which begins on page 77. Meanwhile, following in Chapter 4 are some other techniques you might like to try later.

Wrong side of the block showing the pressing and the rectangles

CHAPTER 4
MORE TECHNIQUES

PIECING - by hand

Our grandmothers did not have the benefits of the rotary cutters. (Some of our mothers did not either!) They had to make their quilts by cutting each piece for each block by hand. Before the middle 1800's all quilts were made by hand. Once the sewing machine was invented, you can bet that quilts were made with that time-saver! Even so, the pieces had to be cut with scissors. To ensure that each piece was the same as the next, our grandmothers made templates to trace. They used whatever they could find, including cardboard from their husbands' new shirt packaging, postcards, catalog covers and eventually cereal boxes.

The problem with the cardboard template is that over time the edges become worn and altered. Eventually the pieces are no longer the same size and inaccuracies occur, which means that the blocks will not fit together well. Have you ever seen an antique quilt, or a photograph of one, that has one side quite a bit longer than the other? My theory is that the templates became distorted and contributed to the lopsided quilt.

Today we are very lucky to have template plastic! Now we can make our templates out of a material that will not alter, unless you hit it with an iron and melt it. And using a Mylar template plastic, made to resist the heat of the iron, can solve even that problem.

The template material of my choice, however, is freezer paper. I have very logical reasons for this that I will be happy to share later. Freezer paper is a product easily purchased in the grocery store. You'll find it either in the freezing and canning section or in the foil and plastic wrap section, depending how your store is laid out. It is relatively inexpensive and the templates made from the paper can be used repeatedly.

Freezer paper is dull on one side and plastic coated on the other. This plastic coating, when placed on your fabric and touched with a heated iron, will temporarily adhere the paper to your fabric. The template stays in place while you trace it and is easily released from the fabric when it is time to stitch. And, the freezer paper template is reusable. Some say you may reuse it up to seven times. I'll be honest, I've used it as many as 20 times and the template still had life!

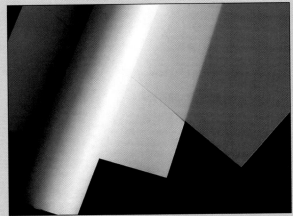

Template materials: freezer paper, template plastic & Mylar

Needles for hand stitching are different from machine needles. Where the larger number indicates a larger machine needle, it is opposite for hand sewing needles. The larger number indicates a smaller needle! It can be very confusing.

Needles come in a variety of styles. There are *betweens*, which are designed for hand quilting. These needles are very short. Since the needle is controlled by your thimble and finger tip and not actually held between your fingers, you will find that the shorter the needle, the more control you will have.

Sharps are a little longer than betweens and are more suited to hand piecing and appliqué. You guide the sharp while holding it between your fingers and only use a thimble to push it through the fabric. A lower number will give you a fatter needle with a larger eye. It is my experience that it is actually easier to stitch with the thinnest needle I can thread. So I stitch with a number 11. There is a number 12, but I have trouble seeing the eye, let alone threading it!

Even longer than a sharp is a *straw* needle, sometimes called a *milliner*. When I appliqué, I don't wear a thimble because it hampers my control. I use a straw needle to appliqué. Since it is longer, the needle does not poke my finger like the sharp does.

While hand piecing, you will, most likely, want to wear a thimble to protect your middle finger of your dominant hand. Unlike appliqué stitching, you will likely load more than one stitch at a time onto your needle when you hand piece. You'll need the thimble to push the needle through the fabric. A well-fitted thimble is invaluable. Today you will find quite an array of styles and materials. You will find leather thimbles, leather thimbles with metal pads, metal thimbles, metal thimbles fitted with a magnet in the tip, plastic thimbles, open thimbles for those of you with long fingernails, rubber thimbles, ceramic thimbles and even fur thimbles (not readily available unless you live in Alaska, though)! Prices of thimbles are equally varied. If you put the thimble on your finger, hold your hand pointing to the floor and shake and the thimble does not fall off, you've probably found the right size. I recommend that you visit your favorite quilting supply store and try them on.

Different thimble styles

Now let me tell you why I like freezer paper for my templates and we'll get started with a hand-pieced block.

We quilters are a unique bunch. We habitually take a perfectly good piece of fabric, cut it up into small pieces and sew it all back together again. By combining it with other fabrics and interspersing a variety of shapes, we create patterns. We make blocks of pattern that we combine with other blocks of pattern and sew the blocks together to create a quilt top.

I look at the block as a puzzle. I want my pieces to go back together exactly so that I don't have any holes in my puzzle. If I have a hole, I have to work to fill it. We don't add more fabric, we kind of stretch what we have and hope it fills the hole. Now, if I trace the shapes of the puzzle individually, I tend to edit. We all do it! Only a machine is less likely to change the lines. Add a pair of scissors to the mix, where we edit again, and we are very likely to end up with a bunch of puzzle pieces that just don't quite fit together, full of holes!

Now, if I draft a line drawing of my block and then cut on the lines, I create the templates that will fit together! Even if I alter the lines a bit in my cutting, I alter them equally from puzzle piece to puzzle piece and they will still all fit together. I could use the template plastic, but I find it much easier to cut the freezer paper. And by ironing the template directly on the fabric, I know it won't slip while I'm tracing the template and my pieces are very accurate. Seam allowance is added in the fabric around the template. Our foremothers sometimes added the seam allowance to the template.

Sawtooth Star block

Let's hand piece a Sawtooth Star block to learn the technique. Remember which one it is?

Begin by cutting a piece of the freezer paper about 9" x 9" square. We are going to make a 6 1/2" x 6 1/2" block (6 inches finished) to learn the technique. If you like, you may use it as the label for the back of your Sampler quilt. (See page 101 for information about the label and how important it is!)

With your 12 1/2" square ruler, trace the top and side of a 6" square. Draw on the non-shiny side of the paper. You can use a pencil that can be erased or a pen if you are very confident. Either one will work on this side of the freezer paper. However, I recommend drawing with a mechanical pencil so that the width of the drawn line doesn't vary. Here, I've used a red marker for clarity. Turn the paper 180 degrees and, aligning the drawn line with the 6" vertical and horizontal marks on your ruler, trace the top and side edges of your ruler.

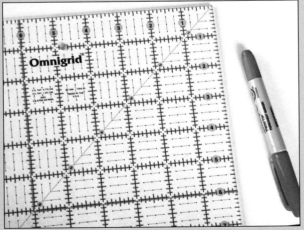

Drawing second line

Exactly 1 1/2" from each of the outside edges, draw

a parallel line inside the square. You should have four corner squares that are 1 1/2" x 1 1/2" and four rectangles on the sides that measure 1 1/2" x 3". The center square should be 3" x 3".

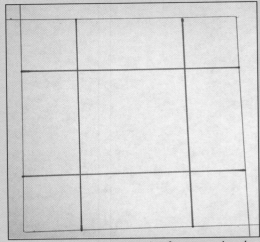

1 1/2" from outside edge

Find the exact middle of each of the sides of the 3" x 3" square and make a little mark. Draw a diagonal line in the rectangles from that half-way mark diagonally to an outside corner of the rectangle. Repeat in the other direction. You will have created a V in each of the rectangles. Do you see the star? It should look just like the Sawtooth Star you made in chapter 3. (Directions beginning on page 54.)

Once I have drawn my block I like to make some notations on it to remind me of various bits of information that won't be so obvious to me after I have cut the pieces apart. To begin with, I want to mark the outside edges so that I can recognize them when I have all the parts cut apart. So I make an X on the line. When the line is cut I'll be left with a little arrow that points to the outside edge. Once the template is removed for stitching, the mark will go with the template. So I transfer the mark in the seam allowance as well.

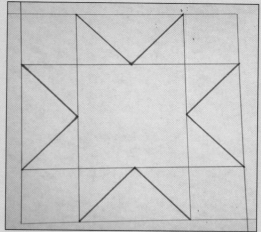

Points drawn

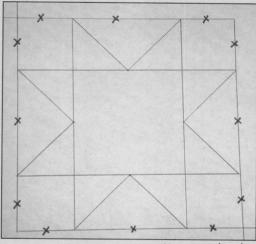

X on outside edge

I also want to mark the straight of grain. In order to avoid distortion, we want the outside edges of our blocks to be on the straight of grain whenever possible. So I draw an arrow that shows me the direction of straight of grain. I do this in each piece. The outside edges of the side rectangles all get an arrow parallel to the edge. The corner squares get an arrow along one edge (If the one edge of a square is on the straight of

grain, they all are) as well as the center square. I mark one of the short sides of the triangles with an arrow. Remember when we sewed those triangles in our sampler? The longest sides of the triangles were bias edges.

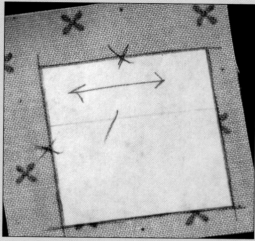

X in the seam allowance

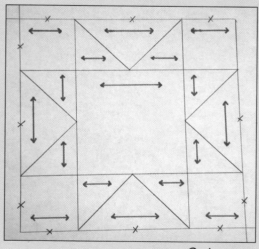

Grain arrows

Then I number the pieces. I want to remember which pieces get sewn to which pieces. Remember, if I alter a line between two pieces, I alter both pieces equally. I want to be sure that I sew those pieces together exactly as the templates were cut apart. I begin in the upper left corner and number from left to right on each of the rows. I always make a little thumbnail sketch of the block, too, and number that the exact same way so that I have a reference when I have everything cut apart. It's my "map" while I'm piecing.

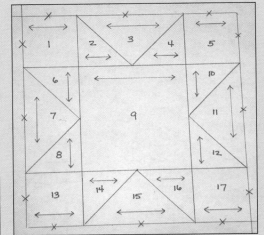

Numbering along with a thumbnail sketch with numbers

The last thing I do is mark an X in the center of each template of the star. These are the templates I am going to iron onto the star fabric. The rest of the templates, the ones with no X in the center, will be ironed onto my background fabric. (Another method to easily show which template is the background and which is not is to circle the number on the template that is the main fabric.) If you think you would like to use the block being described here as a label on the back of your sampler quilt that you began making in chapter 3, you might consider making the star out of a very light fabric on which you can write with a permanent marker and the background out of a dark fabric that will make the star really show up!

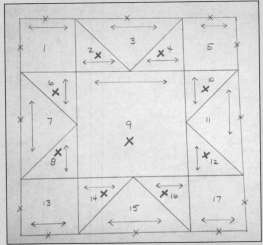

X's for focus fabric

Now we're going to cut it apart very carefully. I like to use my rotary cutter and rotary cutting ruler for this step. This way I know that my edges will be very straight. Align the edge of the ruler with the outside edges of the block and trim away the excess. Begin by cutting the first lines you drew 1 1/2" inside the block, horizontally and vertically. Cut the diagonal lines in the side rectangles next. Separate the templates into two piles, the ones with the X in the center and ones without.

On the ironing board I arrange my two fabrics, wrong side up. Lay the templates with the X on the wrong side of the star fabric so that the arrows that denote the straight of grain are aligned with the straight of grain of the fabric. You may place the templates close together, but not any closer than 1/2". Unless you are conserving fabric, I would recommend that you space them even farther apart. You must leave enough fabric between the templates to account for a 1/4" seam allowance. The edges of the templates with the marks that indicate the outside edge can use a little extra fabric. Allow a full inch between pieces. I give the outside edge extra fabric so that when I have completed the hand stitching and pressing, I can trim my block with my rotary cutter and square ruler so that it is exactly square.

Iron the paper templates to the wrong side of the fabric with a hot dry iron. Steam will distort the paper. It may even shrink it. I suggest that you begin by setting your iron to the wool setting. If your iron runs on the hotter side, the wool setting will be hot enough. If your iron runs cool, the wool setting will not be hot enough. You will know if the iron is hot enough if the freezer paper actually stays attached to the fabric. A cooler iron will not melt the wax enough to adhear the paper to the fabric. But if your iron is too hot, the wax will melt into the fibers instead of onto the surface of the fibers. If that happens, the paper is more difficult to remove and may even peel off in layers, leaving the wax layer on the fabric.

With my rotary cutter and ruler, I cut my pieces from the fabric. I place the 1/4" mark (that is, the mark closest to the cutting edge of the ruler, 1/4" from it) on the edge of the template. When cut, the template shapes have an added 1/4" all the way around the shape.

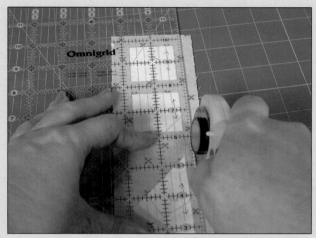
Rotary cutting fabric around templates

Now you have to draw a stitching line around each of the templates, on the wrong side of the fabric. You will do this by tracing the template while it is still attached to the fabric. Choose a marker according to the light or dark value of the fabric. See page 13 for a review of markers.

Templates on fabric before cutting

Tracing with template between hand and marker

Place the fabric pieces on a sandpaper board. If you don't have a sandpaper board or are unable to find one at your quilting supply store, you may use a sheet of medium fine sandpaper. The sandpaper grips the fabric and keeps it from shifting and sliding under your marker, dislodging the freezer paper.

Because the freezer paper can be so easily separated from the fabric, your method of tracing will be a little different than you are probably used to. Instead of holding the marker against the paper so that the marker is between your hand and the edge of the freezer paper, you're going to trace over the top of the paper. That is, the freezer paper is between your hand and the marker. Make the finest line you can manage so that your stitching will be accurate.

Last, I stack my pieces in the numbered sequence, beginning with number one on top. Now I'm ready to begin stitching.

Quilter's knot

Several types of needle threaders

Thread a needle with cotton thread. The color can match one or the other of your fabrics or can be a neutral that blends with the two. I use 60-weight machine embroidery cotton thread (see page 11) and a #11 sharp (see page 58). Did you know that there is a front door and a back door to a needle? The way the eye is stamped into the needle causes a concave side and a convex side. The concave side is the front door. If you can't get the thread to go into the eye of the needle, turn the needle over and try again.

If you have trouble threading the needle no matter what you try to do, I want to tell you that there are several threaders on the market to help you! Be sure to check with your quilting supply store for one. I especially like the desk-style needle threader. I don't even have to be able to see the eye of the needle to get it threaded. The threader does the work!

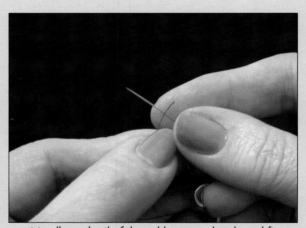

Needle and tail of thread between thumb and finger

Once you have your needle threaded, you are ready to knot the end. I always knot the end I cut from the spool. There is a twist in thread and as it is drawn through the fabric, the twist can become even more tightly twisted, causing the thread to knot while you stitch, if you draw the thread in the wrong direction. By knotting the end you cut, you will eliminate most of those pesky knots.

To knot the thread, hold the needle between your thumb and index finger. Lay the very end of the thread over the needle and hold it between your thumb and index finger. With your other hand, wrap the end of the thread that you're holding around the needle two or three times and hold that between your thumb and index finger.

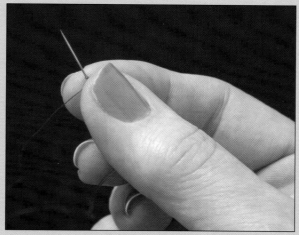

Thread tail wrapped around needle

Without letting go of the thread that you have between your thumb and index finger, draw the needle through your fingers and continue pulling, holding the needle at the eye so you don't lose your thread, until you have pulled the full length of thread through your fingers. You will feel a little knot on the end as it passes from your fingers.

Hand stitching

You will begin by stitching piece #1 to piece #2 on the line that connects the two shapes. You first need to align the two edges so that one traced line is exactly on top of the other line. Because you cannot see through the fabric, you will need to use some tricks to line it up. Don't count on the edge of the fabric. If you were not extremely consistent and accurate when you rotary cut the seam allowances, the traced lines will not line up exactly.

Place a pin straight down into the corner of piece #1 at the beginning of the sewing line, just as you did when matching your intersecting seams while machine piecing. (See page 30 for a review.) The same pin then goes into the corresponding point on piece #2. With another pin, match the other end of the sewing line in exactly the same way. And place a third pin somewhere in the center on the line. With these three pins in place, straight in, place a pin just to the side of the first pin in the seam allowance,

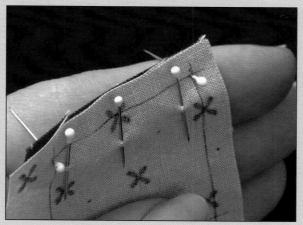

Pinning

this time pinning through both layers as you usually do, taking a very small bite. Place another pin on the other end in the same way and one to the side of the center pin. Then remove the placement pins and you are ready to sew.

Poke the needle through both layers of fabric, right on the line, travel forward and then through both layers again. Before pulling the needle, check the other side to make sure that your stitch is on both the top and bottom lines. If you are satisfied, pull the needle and thread through. Since this is the first stitch, you want to make sure that your knot is secure, so take a second stitch in exactly the same place as the first. The next three or four stitches are fed onto the needle without pulling the thread all the way through.

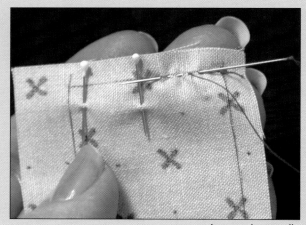

4 stitches on the needle

Check to make sure that the stitches are exactly on both lines and then pull the needle all the way through. This is called a running stitch. Try to make your stitches rather small, say no more than 1/8" in length, shorter if you can do it. Take another set of three or four stitches, but start at the beginning of the last stitch you took. This backstitch

helps to reinforce the seam. If the thread does break at some point, this extra stitch will keep the whole seam from coming apart.

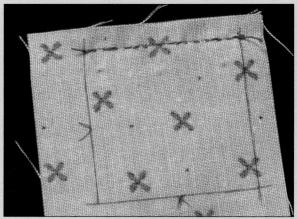

Seam sewn showing the backstitches

Continue in this manner until you reach the end of the seam. To tie off, take a backstitch over the last stitch. Just as you are about to pull the thread all the way through the fabric, pass the needle through the loop of thread twice and then continue to pull. This makes a very secure but tiny knot. Continue to build the block by adding each piece in this manner.

Once you get really comfortable with this technique, you will be able to add successive pieces without tying off and beginning again. By passing through a previous seam allowance with your needle and thread you will be able to begin again on the other side with just a backstitch and no knots. Your block's seams will be more secure.

The only trick to hand piecing is to remember that when you get to an intersecting seam, you do not catch the seam allowance in your stitching. When you get to the intersecting seam, take a backstitch, pass through the stitching of the intersecting seam, take a backstitch on the other side and continue stitching. The seam allowances are all left free.

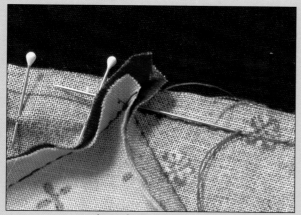

Passing through an intersecting seam allowance

Once the entire block is stitched, you press the seam allowances. Leaving the seam allowances unhindered allows you to press the seam allowances in any direction that seems correct for this block. (Remember to listen to the block!)

After the block is pressed, you can trim it to an exact 6 1/2" x 6 1/2".

HAND APPLIQUÉ

Appliqué is my favorite activity. It is so relaxing. Appliqué is portable and takes very little by way of tools. You need a background, shapes to appliqué, needle and thread to match the appliqué and a small, sharp pair of scissors. OK, I use a few more things than those listed, but once I have my preparation done, I only need the needle, thread, scissors and project.

Every appliqué quilter will have her own favorite methods. A whole book could be written on this subject alone. On these pages, therefore, I will share with you my favorite methods and tools. I encourage you to experiment with as many techniques as you can find and choose the methods that suit you the most.

Tools

When I do appliqué, I favor patterns that show the full-sized drawing of the design. Separated templates for a layered design often don't work for me. By "layered" I mean a design where each shape is bordered by another shape. A design that isn't layered will have shapes that overlap in just one little spot, like a simple posy at the end of a stem. A layered design can have more problems if one isn't accurate in tracing, cutting, stitching. A design that isn't layered provides more leeway in placement without changing the design.

Once I have my design, I trace it onto the template material. If it's a layered design, I trace the design as a complete unit. That way when I cut the shapes apart, the shared lines are identical and will fit back together again. I never add seam allowance to my templates.

There are several choices for templates: template plastic, contact paper, full-page labels, freezer paper. I find freezer paper to be my favorite. I can see through it enough to trace the pattern onto the dull side of the paper. It is reusable because the waxy side adheres to the fabric with enough hold to keep the template from shifting as I trace. It is inexpensive and easily found in most grocery stores, either in the freezing and canning supplies or in the foil wraps. It is easy to cut with a pair of scissors reserved for cutting paper. I iron it onto the right side of my appliqué fabric and it stays put until I release it to stitch.

The markers I use are the same markers discussed on page 13. I use the light chalk marker for dark fabrics and I use the dark marker for light fabrics. The line that I make tracing the template is in the seam allowance and should not show after stitching so this time I don't worry about how thick the line is.

Every appliqué quilter will have his/her favorite thread and good reasons for their choice. Some use silk while others insist that silk is too strong for cotton fabrics and over time will cut the fabric. Others argue that silk thread stretches over time and the stitches loosen. Still others will suggest that by the time the stitches begin to "smile" or the appliqué begins to deteriorate they won't be around anymore and they will have gotten all the enjoyment allotted from the quilts they make. I don't know the ultimate answer and suggest that you experiment and decide what's best for you.

My thread of choice is silk. It blends into the fabric so well that my stitches seem to just disappear. I also use 60-weight cotton thread. A 50-weight piecing thread will not fit through the eye of the needle. Either way, the most important thing is the color. Choose a thread that matches the appliqué, never the background.

Needles, too, are a personal choice. Traditionally appliqué is stitched with a sharp. The numbers 10 -12 are favored the most as they are thin-shafted needles. There are some quilters who use quilting betweens for everything, from appliqué to quilting. This is a very short needle! My favorite is the straw needle. It's a longer needle and I find I get more control with it. I use a #11.

Basting the pieces to the background helps to keep them from shifting while you stitch. Some quilters will baste with thread. That's an extra step I don't like taking, so I baste with pins. Pins come in many lengths. I think that the shorter the pin the better so that as I stitch, my thread doesn't get tangled up in the pins. A 3/4" appliqué pin will work very well. If you insist on using the glass-head quilters pins, be sure to pin from the wrong side of the block. While you stitch on the right side, the pins are well out of the way on the wrong side.

Scissors are as important a tool as your needle and thread. Small scissors with thin sharp points that are sharp all the way to the very end are a must for some of the techniques I'll be showing you later. My favorites are 4" embroidery scissors. They are sharp all the way to the tip and the tips are very thin.

There are a variety of ways to transfer the pattern to your background. If the design is not layered, one can easily "eyeball" placement. Often vertical, horizontal and diagonal finger pressing will be all one needs for placement guides. Some stitchers prefer to trace the design directly onto the background square. By matching the lines on the background with the edge of the appliqué, one can build the design. I must admit that I prefer not to mark the background. I have been known to shift the shapes just enough to miss covering the markings. So I prefer to trace the design onto a clear upholstery vinyl material with a permanent marker. By aligning the overlay with my background square I can easily see where to place my next shape. And if I do shift a bit, no one is the wiser.

Appliqué tools

Preparation

Once I have chosen my appliqué design and gathered my tools I'm almost ready to begin stitching. But there are a few steps of preparation first.

First I trace my design onto the dull side of the freezer paper, numbering the shapes as they are shown on the design. The numbers refer to the stitching sequence. Appliqué stitching occurs from the background forward.

I also extend all of the lines that intersect with another into the next shape. When I cut the shapes apart, these little marks help with placement later. Once the design is on the freezer paper, I trace the design onto the clear upholstery vinyl, making sure to transfer any center and side-center markings as well.

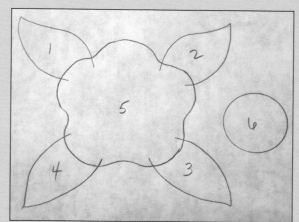

Traced pattern on freezer paper with extending lines

I choose my fabrics for the appliqué before I cut the templates apart. This way I can see the bigger picture and know for sure exactly which fabrics will go where. If I cut the templates apart first, I tend to forget where the pieces go in the design. Once I have chosen the fabrics, I take all the fabrics, my freezer paper pattern and paper cutting scissors to the ironing board. As I cut the templates apart, I lay them on the appropriate fabrics. Place the template on the fabric so that as many of the edges as possible are on the bias. Bias is easier to turn under than the straight grain of the fabric. For a review of bias see page 19.

Once my decisions are made, I iron the templates onto

the right side of the fabric with a dry iron, set on the wool setting. A hotter iron might melt the plastic coating too much and make it sink down into the fibers of the fabric. A cooler iron will not melt the plastic enough to adhere the template to the fabric. Steam will distort the paper.

Using a sandpaper board or a piece of fine sandpaper underneath, I place the appliqué shape on a table and trace. Tracing against the template will very likely loosen the template so I trace over the top of the edge. That is, I keep the template between my hand and the tip of my marker. This is the same way I trace the templates for hand piecing. For a review, refer to page 63.

Once the templates are all traced, I cut my seam allowances. While 1/4" seam allowances are desired for piecing, that really is too much for appliqué and 1/8" is too narrow for many fabrics. I cut my seam allowances 3/16". Once the seam allowances are all cut, I stack the pieces according to the numbering, with number 1 on top, and I'm ready to stitch. Don't remove the paper templates until after placing the shape on your background. Placement will be much easier with the freezer paper still adhered!

Cut your background square larger than you want the finished block to be. I usually add an extra inch. Once the stitching is complete you will trim the block, squaring it to the correct size. Stitching can distort the background. Beginning with an oversized block will eliminate any problems caused by the distortion. Fold the block in half and finger press. Don't iron, as it will

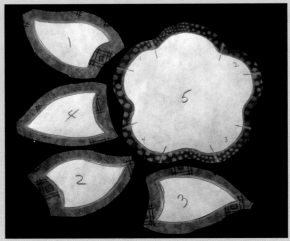

Seam allowance cut

make very permanent creases. Open the block and make a quarter turn and fold again. This time carefully align the first crease. Since the block will be trimmed later, it won't matter if the edges are square. But you want the creases to be perpendicular. These creases will align with the center and side-center markings that you made on the upholstery vinyl overlay.

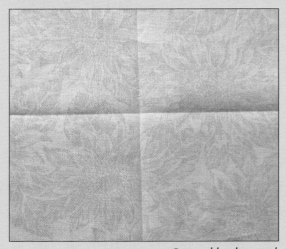

Creased background

Place the overlay over the block, aligning the creases

with the center and side-center markings. With the paper still attached, slide the shape between the overlay (that you're holding in place with your other hand) and the background until the outline of the template matches the outline of the shape on the overlay. When the shape is in place, carefully roll the overlay off. If you lift the overlay, static will probably move your carefully placed appliqué piece, so roll it off carefully.

Using the overlay

Place a few pins in the seam allowance just to secure the shape while you remove the freezer paper. Use a long pin or needle to slide between the paper and the fabric to release the paper without stretching the fabric. When the paper is removed, place pins on the inside of the shape, no closer to the traced line than the width of the seam allowance. Too close to the edge and the pin will prevent the seam allowance from turning under completely. Place the pins in the direction that you will be stitching so that you don't prick your knuckles as you stitch.

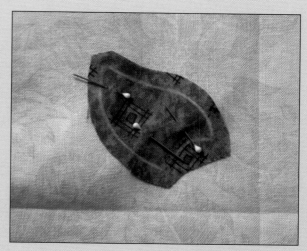

Pins in place

If you are right handed, stitch counter-clockwise around the shape. Left-handers, stitch clockwise.

Stitching

While there are many different methods for getting the seam allowance in place and the shapes attached to the background, I use a method called needle turn. This simply means that I use the tip of my needle to turn under the seam allowance as I stitch. I only turn under as much as can be held in place by my thumbnail until the edge is stitched.

Begin with an 18" length of thread to match the appliqué. Make a quilter's knot. For a review, see page 64. Never begin in a corner unless the corner is going to be overlapped by the next appliqué shape. Instead, begin on a relatively straight place. Bring the needle through the appliqué from behind the traced line to the right side of the appliqué fabric, not through the background.

71

While holding the appliqué in place with your opposing thumb, use the tip of the needle to turn the seam allowance under so that the traced line disappears under the fold. Place the needle into the background just barely under the fold but at the same place the thread is protruding from the fold. Travel forward a tiny bit and then come back up through the background and the fold of the appliqué. Pull the thread taut but not so tight that it puckers. If your stitch begins just under the fold, the stitch disappears as the thread is pulled. If you go into the background next to the fold, your stitch will show, as it will if you come out through the top of the appliqué instead of the side of the fold. I take a second stitch in the same place when I first begin to lock the little knot into the seam allowance.

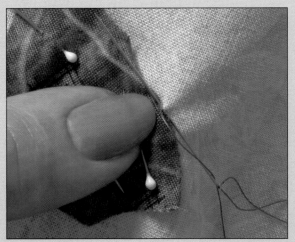

Stitching

When I get to a stopping place or begin to run out of thread, I take a stitch back the way I have just come and then take that last stitch forward again. This forms a figure eight and the thread locks in place. Then I bury the thread in the fold of the appliqué about an inch. The tail is in the fold and there are no knots on the back of my block.

When I'm ready for the next piece, I repeat the process by placing the overlay on the background and placing the appliqué. Once all of the pieces have been appliquéd in place, I'm ready to square up the block.

Place a clean terry cloth towel on your ironing board and place your finished block, right side down, on the towel. Press the block with a hot iron with steam. Remember, press, don't iron!

When you have finished pressing, place the block on your rotary cutting mat. Chances are you will still be able to see your finger-pressed creases enough to be able to center your rotary cutting square ruler on the block. Trim the block the same way you did when you trimmed the center square for your Variable 9-patch block. See page 37 to review.

If you plan to hand quilt your quilt, you may wish to remove the background from behind the appliqué. Very carefully cut the fabric away from behind the appliqué about 1/4" from the stitching. This will eliminate a layer of fabric. You will want to quilt around each of the appliqué shapes to give them some dimension.

MACHINE APPLIQUÉ

Fusing the appliqué to the background is the favored method if you wish to machine stitch the appliqué shapes. A lightweight fusible material is preferred so that the appliqué will be soft. Fusing the appliqué is done in mirror image. So if you don't want the design to be backwards you will need to trace the pattern in reverse. Place the pattern, right side down, on a light box or a sunny window and trace the design onto the reverse side of the pattern or onto a new piece of paper. This will reverse the pattern and it is the reversed pattern that you use.

Fused appliqué does not employ seam allowance. I will suggest, however, that you add just a bit to the edges that are overlapped by another shape so that there are no gaps.

When choosing the fusible material, look for a lightweight, paper-backed fusible. There are products that have the capability of letting you place and replace your shapes before actually fusing. Check with your local quilt shop to see the different products.

Trace the individual appliqué shapes onto the paper side of the fusible. This is not what I recommend for hand appliqué but I have a good reason here, so keep reading. When tracing the shapes, leave about an inch between each shape. Cut the shapes out with your paper-cutting scissors, not on the drawn line but about 1/2" outside the line. This is why you don't trace the design as a whole. You need that 1/2" around each shape.

Once the shapes are roughly cut out, cut a window inside the shape about 1/4" from the traced line.

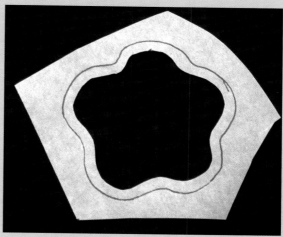

Window

What you will be left with is the outline of the appliqué shape, a "window."

Following the instructions that came with your product, iron the window to the wrong side of the appliqué fabric. Then cut the shape out by cutting on the traced lines.

Once the shapes have been cut out, you may peel the paper from the fabric. What's left is the glue. If you have a very simple design you may fuse the shapes directly to the background block, again carefully following the directions that came with your fusible product.

If you have a layered design, you may want to do a preliminary arrangement and fusing. There is a product that is a sheet of Teflon. This sheet is opaque and will release the hold of the fusible material without harming the fusing properties. Place the design on the surface of your ironing board. Place the sheet of Teflon over the pattern. You will be able to see the design.

Lay the appliqué shapes on the sheet using the pattern underneath as a guide.

Fusible appliqué works the same as hand appliqué in that the sequence works from background forward. When you are satisfied with the arrangement, touch the iron to the appliqué to fuse. Let it cool and carefully peel the entire arrangement off of your Teflon sheet and place it on your background square. When you are satisfied, fuse the arrangement to the background. Again, I recommend that the background be larger than the finished block should be. The directions that came with your fusible material will tell you how hot the iron should be.

Fusible on appliqué sheet

The fusing is only temporary. To secure the appliqué to the background you must stitch. This is where the sewing machine comes in. I use an open-toed embroidery foot on the machine and I move the needle to the right so that the toe of the foot, on your right, travels right next to the raw edge of the appliqué. I use a needle that is the finest that my thread will accommodate. Whatever

stitch you use on your machine, the idea is to cover the raw edge of the appliqué. Some quilters prefer a satin stitch in a contrasting or matching thread. Some quilters will use a simple zigzag stitch or a decorative stitch. Some quilters have machines that will duplicate a hand buttonhole stitch. Only your machine limits you.

Before stitching, consider backing your block with a stabilizer. A stabilizer will keep the fabric from bunching while stitching, leaving the block smooth.

There are several stabilizer materials on the market. Some easily tear away after stitching. Some even disappear if you add water. Your local quilt shop will have some choices. If you wish, you could iron a piece of freezer paper onto the back of the block. The only drawback is that the stitching is through the paper as well as the fabric and will have to be picked out. Unless, that is, you are making a wall hanging. In that case you may leave the paper under the stitching with no problem.

Choose your stitch and thread and begin stitching around the edge of the appliqué shapes. Begin with the shape that is closest to the background. Just as in hand appliqué, the stitching sequence is from background forward.

Complete the stitching and remove the stabilizer. At this point you may need to square up the block.

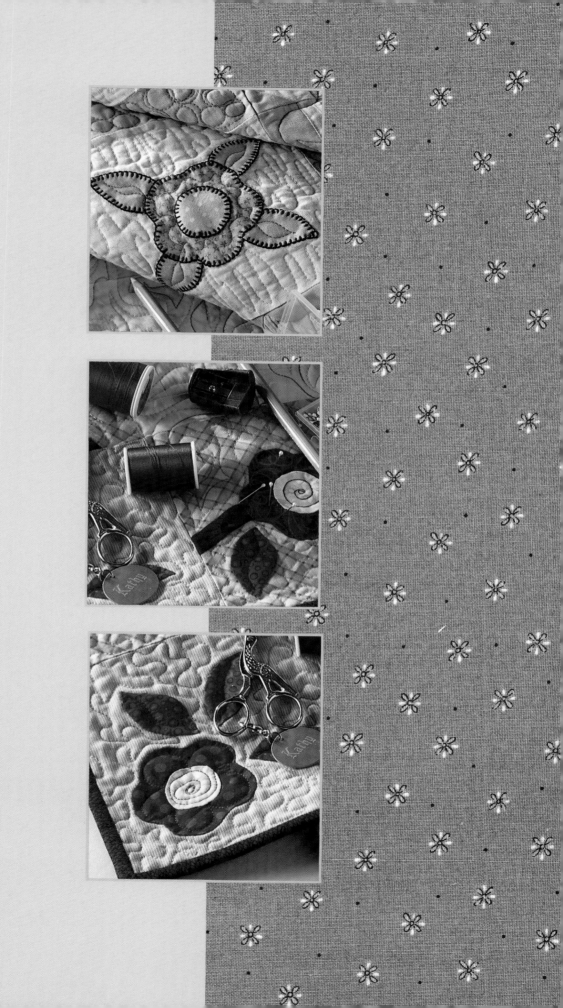

CHAPTER 5
FINISHING YOUR QUILT

SASHING

Sometimes referred to as lattice, the sashing of a quilt top is the grid that separates the blocks. Sometimes the sashing is pieced and looks like it is part of the blocks. Sometimes it is pieced and clearly separate from the blocks. Sometimes it is very simple.

There are several styles of sashing but I think the most basic sashing entails two elements, sashing and corner stones. The corner stones are squares that are formed at the intersections of vertical and horizontal sashing strips.

The sashing strips will appear between each of the 16 sampler blocks and also surround the blocks to act as a first border. You will need (40) 2 1/2" x 9 1/2" rectangles from your sashing fabric and (25) 2 1/2" x 2 1/2" squares from your corner stone fabric.

Begin by cutting (3) 9 1/2" wide strips from your sashing fabric, cutting across the grain from selvage to selvage. Turn the strips a quarter turn and remove the selvages, making sure that you are cutting perfectly perpendicular to the long edge. Cut (16) 2 1/2" strips from two of the 9 1/2" wide pieces and (8) 2 1/2" strips from the third.

Cut (2) 2 1/2" wide strips from your corner stone fabric, cutting across the grain from selvage to selvage. Turn the strips a quarter turn and remove the selvages, making sure that you are cutting perfectly perpendicular to the long edge.

Cut (16) 2 1/2" squares from one strip and (9) 2 1/2" squares from the other.

All of your sewing is, again, with consistent 1/4" seam allowances. Sew a 2 1/2" x 9 1/2" strip to the left side of each of your blocks. Press the seams to the sashing strips.

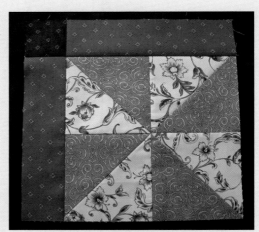

Square/sashing unit sewn to top of block

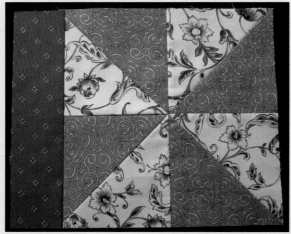

Sashing on left of block

Sew a 2 1/2" x 2 1/2" square to one end of 24 sashing strips. Press the seams to the sashing strips.

Sew a square/sashing unit to the top of each of the blocks, snugging the

intersecting seams and pressing the seams to the square/sashing unit.

Arrange your blocks in four rows of four blocks each. Move them around until you are satisfied, or take a look at my Sampler on page 26 or 79. Consider that the blocks are numbered 1-4 on the top row (row #1) with

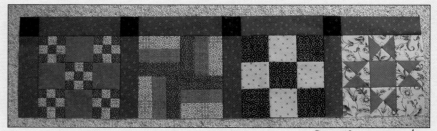

Row #1 sewn together

Square/sashing unit

#1 being the first block on the left. Sew block #2 to the right side of block #1. Sew block #3 to the right side of block #2. Sew block #4 to the right side of block #3. Sew a square/sashing unit to the right side of block #4. Each time you add a block, press the seams to the sashing strips.

Repeat the same sewing sequence for row #2 and row #3.

Sew a square/sashing unit to the bottom of each of the blocks you have chosen for row #4, snugging the intersecting seam allowances. Press the seam allowances to the newly added square/sashing units.

Sew the squares in the same sewing sequence that you followed for rows #1-3. Add the last block/sashing unit to the right side of block #4. Press all of the seam allowances to the sashing.

All blocks sewn together

Sew row #2 to the bottom of row #1. Because some of your seams are pressed in opposite directions, you should be able to snug some of the intersecting seams. I advise that you pin the intersections using your favorite method. See page 30 to review pinning. Continue sewing the rows to the bottom of the previous section, pressing the seams to the previous row.

BORDERS

The outer border is the final frame for your quilt top.

This is the last step before quilting and can make or break a quilt. If the border is not put on correctly, your quilt will not lie flat or hang straight. It is very important that you measure your quilt top at this point to determine the length of the borders. While the calculator may tell you that your Sampler quilt top should measure 46 1/2" x 46 1/2" at this point, any number of reasons could point to it measuring less or even more!

Borders can be a solid strip of fabric (as on the "4-Patch Strip" quilt on page 104), pieced (as on the "Sweet Magnolia" quilt shown on page 144), mitered in the corner, or a block at the corner (as in the "Rail Fence a Bloomin" quilt on page 128), appliquéd (as on the "Rail Fence a Bloomin" quilt), or a combination. Sometimes it will be the center of the quilt that will tell you what type of border to use and sometimes it will be the border fabric that will suggest the style. You will find directions for making the different styles with the projects listed above. My border for the sampler is the mitered style because the fabric I used just begged for it! Remember, you have to listen to your fabric.

Begin by measuring through the vertical center of your quilt top. If you just measure the edges, you may find that some distortion has taken place. Sewing the border on will result in a wavy border. So always measure through the center.

To make the strips of your border, fold your fabric in half the length of the fabric so that the selvage edges are aligned on one side and a fold on the other, straightening the fabric as described on page 20. With your

6" x 24" ruler, remove the selvages. If your fabric is straight, you can align the ruler with the selvage edge. I recommend that you remove an inch or so. The width of the selvage (the tighter weave than the rest of the yardage on the edges), varies in width from fabric to fabric.

Sometimes it looks like the selvage is just 1/2" wide. Sometimes it can be as much as an inch. You'll have plenty of fabric if you remove an inch or a little more. If you are using a fabric with a stripe print as in my Sampler quilt, let the design tell you how wide to cut your strips. Use the line of the print to guide your cutting.

Once the selvages are removed, you can cut 6" strips through both layers, the length of the fabric, cutting both of the side borders at once. Your strips should be as long as the measurement you found for the middle of your quilt top. For a mitered corner, you will need the strips to be as long as the measurement, plus the width of the two border strips, and then add a couple of inches for good measure.

Find the center of the strip by folding the strip in half lengthwise and mark with a pin. On the mitered border you will also have to find the point that the quilt top corners will match. Simply measure from the center toward the end until you have reached half the measurement of the quilt top. Repeat in the other direction. Place a pin to represent the corners. Find the center of the two halves by folding in quarters and mark. Find the center of the sides of the quilt top and mark with a pin. Find the center of the two halves the same way and mark. Now

match the pin marks and pin the strips to your quilt top, right sides together, to the sides of your quilt top. Sew with a 1/4" seam allowance, beginning and ending 1/4" from the ends, and press the seam allowance toward the strip.

Measure the horizontal middle of your quilt top with the borders added. This is the length to cut the top and bottom borders plus a couple of inches for good measure. Cut the strips as you did the first set of strips.

Find the center of the strips and the quilt top edges in the same way you did the sides and mark. Place a pin at the other points just as you did before. Pin the borders to the top and bottom sides of the quilt top as you did the sides and sew with a 1/4" seam allowance, beginning and ending 1/4" from the corners of the quilt top. Again, press the seams to the borders.

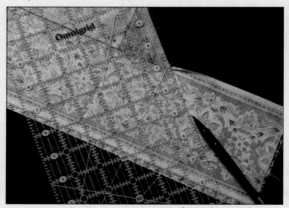

Marking the 45 degrees

Now you're ready to work on the corners. I always work this next step on my ironing board so that I can use the iron. With right sides together, fold the quilt top diagonally, lining up the top edge with the right edge. Perfectly align the seams that attach the borders, placing a few pins along the seams to secure. Place a long ruler on the diagonal fold, extending it over the border strips. With a pencil, trace a line on the border strips that exactly extends the line of the fold. This line will be 45 degrees from the outside edge of the border. Place a few pins across the line to secure against slippage when you move the quilt top to your sewing machine.

Fold back the seam allowance that is between the quilt top and the border to expose the beginning point of the previous seams. You will sew right on the line that you drew. I find that if I begin sewing at the seam out to the corner, the corner will stretch slightly. I suggest that you begin at the outside corner and sew toward the seam, stopping right at the seam and not catching the seam allowance. When you have sewn to the seam, backstitch a couple of stitches to secure.

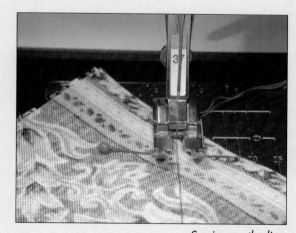

Sewing on the line

Back at the ironing board, open the seam you just stitched and press. Trim the excess fabric so that you are left with a 1/4 inch seam allowance. Press the inside corner flat. Repeat this sequence for the remaining three corners.

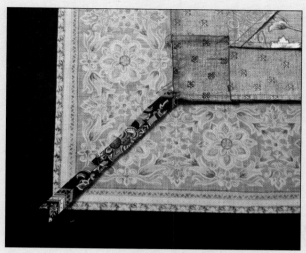

Wrong side of the mitered corner

Your quilt top is now ready for the quilting!

QUILTING

Measure your top horizontally and vertically. Add another 4-8 inches and that is the size that your backing needs to be. Often you will have to piece the backing as there are very few fabrics more than 44 inches wide. Your local quilt shop, however, may have some fabrics that are designed to be backing and will be as much as 108-110 inches wide. If you have to piece the backing, consider whether your quilt will be hanging on a wall or decorating your bed. When making a quilt to hang on the wall, it is recommended that the seam you have to put on the back travel from top to bottom as opposed to horizontally. And the vertical grain of the backing should be from the full length of the fabric instead of from selvage to selvage. There is less give in the length. This means that the fabric, hanging on the wall, is less likely to sag. You probably don't have to worry as much about the grain if your quilt will be on a bed instead. And never use a bed sheet as the backing for your quilt. The thread count of sheet material is so high that it is very difficult to pass the needle through. The difficulty will take all the fun of quilting out of your project!

Most patterns include the direction, "Quilt as desired." I have a theory about that sentence. There are so many quilters who feel that quilting is driven by rules. I am just enough of a maverick that I like to think that the quilting stage is the one place you can forget the rules! You get to do anything you want to! You may decide to test your finest hand quilting with quilting thread or you may decide that the longer stitches you create with perle cotton thread would be perfect to enhance your piecing. You can create feathered wreaths or simple posies over the surface of your quilt top or you can quilt an overall grid that gives the impression of more piecing. You are only limited by your imagination! Let your personal taste be your guide and quilt as desired!

There are a few things, however, that you need to consider to make the job easier and for the outcome to be a success.

Marking

If you think you'd like to "draw pictures" with your quilting, chances are you would like to make sure that those pictures are evenly spaced, are consistent in size and shape and, over all, even. To do that, you will need to mark the design in some way.

At your quilting supply store you will find a wonderful variety of stencils. Stencils are designs that are cut into a plastic sheet. The designs are there by way of channels that guide your marker as you draw the design on your quilt top. The designs run the gamut from simple grids to floral designs to simple or elaborate feather wreaths. You are certain to find something that will suit you.

Quilting stencils

Once you decide on the design, you will need to choose the marker with which to draw the design. There are graphite markers, water-soluble markers, soapstone markers, chalk markers and variations of each. Every quilter will tell you her favorite and swear by it. The quilting supply stores are loaded with every type of marker made.

I wish I could tell you that so-and-so marker is THE marker to use, that it will be easy to apply and will wash out every time. I wish I could tell you that, but unfortunately, I cannot. Just when I find a marker that seems to work, I use it on a different fabric and it doesn't wash out at all. So, the best advice I can give you is to test every marker on every fabric before you use it on your quilt top. A marker that works on your first quilt may not work on your second because you are using a different fabric. So read the directions that come with your marker carefully and test first! And mark with a light hand. A heavy mark is going to be more difficult to get out. You may even have to re-mark sections as you work, or you might consider marking sections as you quilt. I know quilters who work both ways.

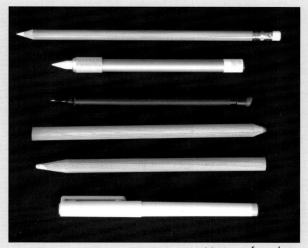

Variety of markers

There is one marker that I do want to make extra comments about and that is the blue water-soluble marker. Adding water to the marks makes the marks seem to disappear. A simple misting will make you believe that the marks are gone. If you remember nothing else, remember this; the chemicals are still there. To remove the water-soluble marks, first soak the finished quilt in cool water for a good 20 minutes. Then wash the quilt in cool water, rinsing thoroughly. Only then will the marks be truly gone. If you just mist, the marks will return. And the returning marks may not wash out.

So soak and then wash, rinsing thoroughly.

Water-soluble markers are also very heat sensitive. Heat will set the marks permanently, so never iron the quilt top after marking it. And don't leave the marked quilt in a hot car or hot storage area, such as an attic, for very long. The heat will set the marks and no amount of washing will help. And remember, too, washing in hot water will not remove the marker but set the marker. I cannot emphasize too much the importance of reading and following the directions that come with your marker.

An alternative to marking a design on the quilt top is to use masking or painter's tape as a straight guide. The tape is movable and reusable. Machine stitching or hand quilting can be done with the tape as a guide. There are a variety of tape widths. The quilting supply store even has 1/4" wide tape, one plain and one marked with lines to help you make evenly spaced stitches as well as stitches consistent in length. If you like, you can find 1/8" wide tape at automobile detailing stores.

Variety of masking tapes

Your sewing machine's walking foot also has an attachment, a spacer bar that guides you in consistently spaced rows of quilting.

Batting

The middle layer of your quilt is the batting. Your batting layer needs to be larger than your quilt top but does not need to be as large as your backing. Ideally, the batting will be about 2-3 inches larger than your top on all sides.

It is the batting that gives your quilt the dimension when you stitch through all three layers; the top, batting and backing. The type of batting you choose will determine how closely you quilt, how you wash and dry your quilt, even how you will use the quilt. There are polyester battings, cotton battings and blends. There are even wool battings and silk battings.

Packaged batting

Harriet Hargrave is probably THE foremost expert on batting and even she cannot tell you which batting you

should use. She uses a variety of battings, all determined by the quilting she plans, whether hand or machine, and the use the quilt will enjoy. There are a few guidelines I can give to you, but you are really going to want to investigate on your own.

Some 100% cotton battings may be more difficult to hand quilt than a polyester batting. Some polyester battings may have too high a loft (depth) to hand quilt. A cotton/poly blend may not give your quilt that "old" look you desire. A cotton batting will make the quilt more comfortable than a polyester batting. The polyester batting will not breathe so don't use it for a baby quilt. A wool batting cannot be dried in the automatic dryer so must be laid flat to dry. A silk batting is very expensive. Batting comes on a roll and in individual packages. Confused yet?

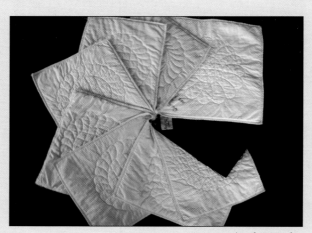

Batting/quilt samples

When you visit your quilting supply store, please ask for recommendations from the staff and read the packaging to give you hints about the individual types of batting. The quilting store where I work has samples of different batting quilted into little muslin "quilts." You might ask if your quilting supply store has something similar. These samples let one see what effect the batting has on the overall look of the quilt.

Basting threads and needles

Before quilting the quilt top, batting and backing must be basted together. If you will be machine quilting you will probably want to use safety pins to baste. Hand quilting encourages thread basting so that your quilting thread won't get hung up on the pins as you are stitching. Either method, you begin the same.

I do not enjoy crawling around on the floor, so I always baste my quilts on top of a table. Place your backing fabric, wrong side up, on the tabletop. If your table isn't large enough for the whole quilt to fit, you may baste in sections, beginning with the middle. To secure and stretch the backing, I use masking tape if the backing is going to fit the table, or heavy-duty clips from the office supply store if I'm basting in sections.

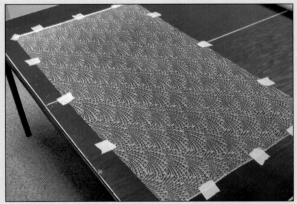

Backing stretched

As you secure the backing, you will be working from side to opposite side until you're finished. Begin at the center of one of the sides. Tape to the tabletop or clip the edge. On the opposite side, in the center, give the fabric a little tug to stretch and tape or clip. On the center of a third side, give the fabric a little tug to stretch and tape or clip. On the opposite side, in the center, repeat. Return to the first side and give the edge a little tug to one side of the tape or clip that is there and tape or clip. Repeat on the other side of the first tape or clip. On the opposite edge, do the same thing and then go to the third side and repeat. Repeat on the fourth side. Go back to the first side and tape or clip again, working to the corner. Depending on the size of the quilt, you may only need 5 pieces of tape or 5 clips per side. Keep working on opposite sides until you have taped or clipped the whole piece of backing fabric.

Spread your batting over the center of the backing fabric. You won't have to do much to stretch the batting. I use my whole forearm and hand to spread the batting from the center out. You don't need to stretch as much as remove wrinkles. If you are using the clips, transfer the clips so that they include the batting as well as the backing. Once you have smoothed the batting you are ready to add the quilt top.

Again, smooth the top over the batting from the center out. Be sure that you have removed any loose threads that may shadow through the top when you're finished. If you don't get them now they are there forever. You do not need to clip the top as you did the batting and backing if you are using clips, and you don't secure it with tape.

Thread basting is done with a long needle, a basting needle, and a light colored thread. You may use any thread you have. I use a spool of white polyester thread that I have had forever. I suggest using white or a very light color so that over time the dye from the thread has no chance of staining your quilt top. Start with a very long piece of thread, say 10 feet, and thread it onto a basting needle. I wrap the thread around a little card, usually reserved for embroidery floss, but you could use a 3" x 5" card cut into fourths. Thread as many needles in this manner as you have in your needle package. Threading multiple needles keeps you from having to stop regularly to rethread your needle, saving you time.

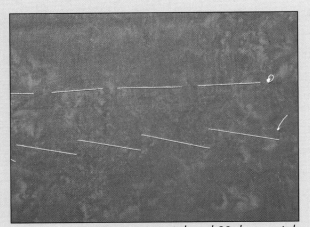

Basting running stitch and 90-degree stitch

Knot one end of the thread. You will be working with a single strand as you baste. Begin in the center and work out to each of the four corners. Basting is done with a running stitch, a very long running stitch. I usually take a 1/2" long stitch about every two or three inches. Other quilters will take a 1/2" stitch but at a 90-degree

angle. The photograph shows both styles of stitch. If I run out of thread I take several stitches in place to secure. I don't make knots.

After you have a diagonal line of running stitches from the center to all four corners make a line of running stitches from the center to the center of each of the four sides. When you stand back you will notice an X through the center and a + dividing the top into fourths. Now you can go back and stitch rows of running stitches, about every three or four inches, all the way across the quilt sandwich, again beginning in the center and working out to a side.

If you have had to baste your top in sections, shift the top over to one side so the unbasted portion can now be clipped to the top of your table. Baste as you did the center portion.

When you have basted the entire top, roll the backing over the batting on the front and baste, enclosing the batting inside the fabric. This will prevent the batting from snagging and shredding as you quilt.

HAND QUILTING THE SANDWICH

Needles

The first quilt I made was quite a learning experience. The group of ladies that were teaching me to quilt had helped me at every stage: deciding the pattern, choosing the fabric, advice regarding prewashing. When it came to actually quilting, though, I had my own ideas! I took one look at that tiny needle that was given to me and I realized that there was no way I could hold it between my fingers (as I always did when hemming a skirt). So I chose one of my trusty sewing needles, the one I always used to hem my skirts. As I quilted, trying to use the method I was shown, I did have trouble. The ladies had shown me how I was to quilt and I wasn't to "hold" the needle at all. It was the thimble that guided the needle. I actually heard myself say out loud, "If I had a much shorter needle, I'd have much more control!" That's when it hit me that quilting between needles were not just skimpier needles in the metal department. It was designed very short for a reason. In fact, I now realize, the shorter the better!

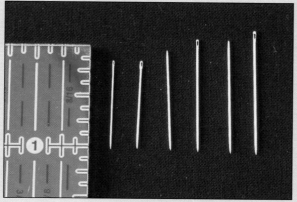

Various sizes of quilting betweens

Some quilting teachers recommend the #9 quilting between as the best to begin with. The numbering is backwards from the sewing machine needles. The smaller number indicates the larger needle. The needle is a little longer and the shaft is a little thicker. In that regard, the needle won't bend quite as easily. But I think that the thicker shaft is a little harder to push through the fabric. If you have trouble, then you'll

want to try the smaller needle; a #11 or #12. You'll have plenty of choices. Some needles will have a slightly larger eye to make it easier to thread. Needles are actually quite personal. The best advice I can give is to decide for yourself. Try a few different needles and then you can settle on the one with which you are most comfortable.

Depending on the thread you use, your needle may need to change. Some of the decorator threads may not work with the same needle you use with your favorite hand quilting thread. Just remember, the larger the number, the smaller the needle and eye. And remember, too, that there are needle threaders to help you. See page 64 for a review.

If your needle begins to bend, you will not be able to make straight stitches. A curve in the needle is a sure signal to get yourself a new needle.

Thread

On the market today are quite a variety of threads. The most common thread for quilting is a heavier cotton thread that has been glazed for ease in quilting. You are not limited to the hand quilting threads, however. Your grandmother would probably have used her normal sewing thread and treated it by drawing a strand through bees wax to cut down on the possibility of knotting and give it added strength. There are new products on the market that you can use like bees wax to treat the thread the same way. Again, I recommend that you experiment and decide with which product you are most comfortable.

Quilting threads and conditionaer

Once you get the hang of quilting, you might like to experiment with different threads. There are a number of threads, from metallics to holographic ribbons to shiny polyesters to rich perle cottons. The most fun you can have is experimenting to see what effects you can achieve with the different threads on the market today.

Thimbles

As with needles, there are different styles of thimbles for different stitching jobs. Traditionally a quilter will wear her thimble on her middle finger of her dominant hand. However, there are quilters who feel that they have more control with their index finger and wear the thimble on that finger. The thimble guides the needle through the fabric as she quilts. The fit of the thimble is important as well is the type of thimble you choose. See page 59 for a review of thimbles.

For quilting, the most common thimble has a flat top with a ridge around the edge. Some quilters prefer to guide the needle with the tip of their thimble. Other quilters feel it is more ergonomically safe to guide the needle with the side of the thimble. If the side is used, then there need to be deep dimples. I must admit that I use my index finger and I use the side of the thimble. I find much less strain on the back of my hand with this method and I'm able to guide the needle with much more accuracy. I hope that you will experiment to find the method and the thimble that works best for you.

Quilting thimbles

Hoops

When our foremothers quilted, a quilt top, batting and backing were stretched on a large frame and a group of women got together to quilt the top in what was called a *bee*. Quilt top making was a solitary activity; the quilting bee provided the companionship and social activity that women still crave today. You may not get your neighbors to all come over and help you quilt your quilt, but you can join a quilting guild, a community of quilters who learn together and often stitch together.

While some quilters still prefer to stretch their quilt sandwich on the large frame, many more opt for the more space-saving hoop. There are many different hoops, from 9" round wooden hoops to floor stand models and all shapes in between. There are square hoops and round hoops and oval hoops. There is even a half-round, designed to be used when quilting the outside border. Every quilter has her favorite. My recommendation is that you choose one no larger than twice the distance from the tip of your finger to the inside crook of your elbow.

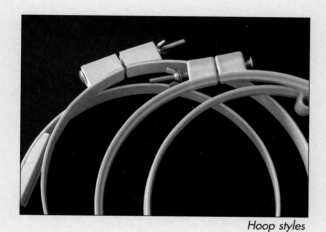

Hoop styles

Anything larger and you'll have a hard time reaching the center of the hoop to work.

You will want your quilt to be slightly loose in the hoop. If you stretch it as tight as a drum, you will not be able to make small, even stitches. As you load your stitches on the needle, you will be rocking the needle from an upright position to a more flattened position against the quilt. If the quilt is too tight in the hoop, you won't be able to rock the needle easily back up to the upright position. You will bend your needle more readily, load

fewer stitches onto the needle at a time and your stitches stand the chance of being uneven.

My favorite hoop has a ridge on the outside surface of the inner ring that fits into a "dent" on the inside surface of the outer ring. Once I have secured the quilt in the hoop it is less likely to shift and loosen even more. Others will say they don't like that hoop for that very reason. Again, you are going to have to try different hoops to find the one you like the best.

The Quilting Stitch

Somewhere along the way, quilters began to worry more about the number of stitches they can make across an inch of surface than the quality of the stitch. By quality I mean consistency. All Master quilters will tell you that the length of the stitch is not nearly as important as how even the stitches are. Naturally you are going to want to strive for the shorter stitches. The shorter stitches will hold the three layers together more securely. Longer stitches can easily get caught on something and get pulled, possibly even break. But worrying about the number of stitches per inch is not a good idea.

I surveyed a number of quilters, asking them, when counting the stitches, are the stitches that show on the top surface counted, the back surface or both? Unfortunately, I could not find a common answer. So, if we don't really know for sure what stitches to count, how can we know just how many stitches we make?! So, don't worry about the number of stitches. Just try to make all the stitches the same, long or short.

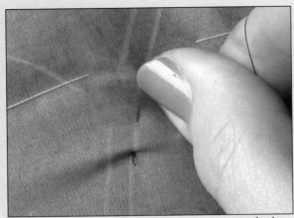

Burying the knot

into the quilt so that you go through the top, into the batting but not out the bottom. The entry point for the needle should be about 1/2 inch from your beginning point, on the design marking. Pull the needle out at the starting point. Give a little tug so that the tiny knot pops through the top and gets stuck in the batting. Make sure that the tail goes all the way into the sandwich.

There are quilters who quilt with what is called a stab stitch. This means that they place the threaded needle straight down into the top, through to the back. With their dominant hand underneath the quilt they turn the

My friend Linda Mooney pointed out one day that sometimes you will want to make longer stitches anyway. Depending on the batting you're using and the fabric, a longer stitch may give a nicer finished look. In all likelihood, a looser woven homespun fabric will not even let your tiny stitches show up. Just strive for consistency and you won't go wrong.

Ok, how do you quilt? Begin by making a quilter's knot at the end of an 18″ length of quilting thread. (See page 64 for a review of the quilter's knot.) Place your needle

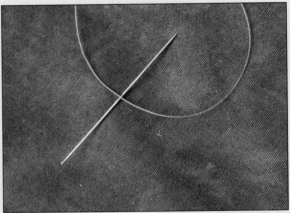

Stab stitch quilting needle

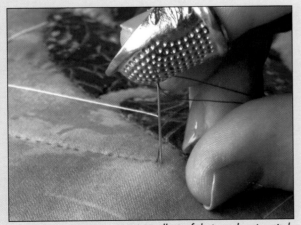

Needle in fabric to begin stitch

needle and attempt to come straight up through the top next to the previous stitch. They pull the thread all the way through and repeat. Most people find this to be very difficult. It is very difficult to make all of the stitches the same length and in a straight line. I once took a class from a local teacher who is an incredible stab stitch quilter. I actually like the process and found that I could get the hang of it. However, it was a pretty slow process. In talking to other quilters, I get the same comments regarding the speed. There is even a needle with points on both ends, and the eye in the middle, so you don't have to flip the needle as you stitch. I hope you try it for yourself!

The more common quilting stitch is the rocking stitch. Your dominant hand places the needle into the top of the quilt sandwich while your other hand is directly underneath with a finger under the needle. I tend to use my index finger, while other quilters use their middle finger. I don't think it makes a difference.

The trick is to poke the needle through so that it penetrates all three layers without also penetrating your finger! The less you prick your finger, the more benefits; your finger will not be sore (well, less sore, anyway), you will draw no blood and your stitches will be consistently shorter. When I quit poking my finger, my quilting suddenly became much better!

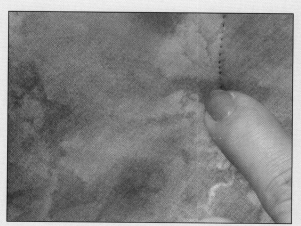
Under side of quilt in hoop showing finger

Once you have penetrated all three layers, lay the needle down flat and go through all three layers again until the point of the needle just pops through to the top,

just until you feel it with the pad of your thumb. Now rock that needle straight up again and repeat. Load stitches onto the needle in this manner until you can no longer stand the needle straight up. You will probably have three or four stitches loaded. Push the needle all the way through until the thread is taut. Then place the point into the quilt top and begin again. The trick is to start your first stitch of a grouping the same distance from your last stitch as the other stitches are from each other. The lengths of the stitches need to be consistent, but so do the spaces in between.

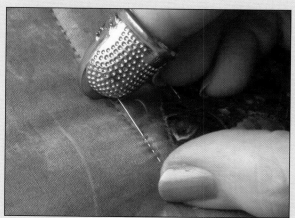
Several stitches loaded onto needle

Remember, too, that your stitches follow your markings. Besides making your stitches even in length, strive to make them straight, one after the other. Angling them gives them an uneven look.

When you reach the end of your thread, you need to tie off in a way that insures that the stitches remain secure. There are several methods. Ultimately, the goal is to secure the end with no knots showing on the front or back of your quilt.

Here's what I do. I take my last stitch. Then I place the point of my needle back into the hole that the thread is poking from, and travel back the way the stitching came, staying within the batting. I weave the needle between a few of the stitches; bring the needle partway out and then push the eye of the needle through the stitches and batting in the opposite direction. The eye is small enough that it will poke easily through the fabric so that I can clip the thread. By weaving the thread through the quilting stitches, the thread becomes secure.

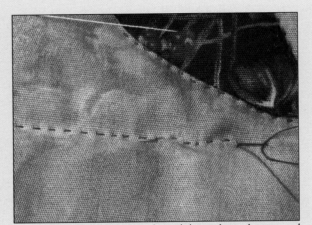

Weaving thread through stitches to end

Other quilters will make a French knot in the thread about 1/2" from the last stitch and then poke the needle into the batting, popping the knot through, just as you did when you began, and then clip the thread. I prefer to weave the thread through the stitches because I have a fear that the knot can pop through again in use.

There is one "rule" that you will want to keep in mind. It is that "quilting should meet quilting." In other words, you will want to make sure that a line of quilting ends at another line. Very rarely will you want to have a line just end, unless you quilt a vein into a leaf or a little

"curl" is in the design. This is a very practical rule, actually. Quilting meeting quilting means more security. The stitches are less likely to break and your quilt stays together through use and washing.

MACHINE QUILTING THE SANDWICH

When you baste the quilt top, batting and backing together before machine quilting, you may use small safety pins. There are several styles on the market. I recommend small pins with a thin shaft. A larger pin will make holes in your fabric that may not disappear.

Pinning on a tabletop can be a bit of a challenge. Using a small spoon to catch the tip of the pin will save your fingers. Your local quilt shop also has a tool that works very well to catch the tip and lift so that you can close the pin easily.

Pin basting with tool

Begin pinning in the center and work out to the edges, pinning about every 3" or a fist's width. As you stitch you will remove the pins as you get to them. If you are working on a very large quilt, you will have to roll or accordion fold the quilt in order to fit it under the arm of your machine. A large table surface will help support the quilt while you work.

If this is your first machine quilting experience, I recommend that you stitch in straight lines. For this you will need the walking foot or even feed foot for your machine. This foot works with your feed dogs with a second set of feed dogs, working on the top layer. Both layers are pushed along at the same time, preventing the top layer from slipping.

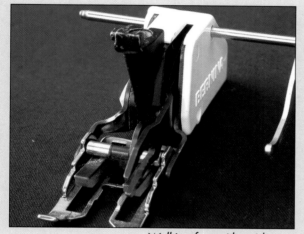

Walking foot with guide arm

The "rule" for hand quilting and machine quilting is the same. That is, quilting should meet quilting. Begin quilting in the center and work out toward the edges. This will go a long way to preventing puckering in the back. Working from the edge to the center could cause some shifting that will definitely catch up with you in the center by way of pleats or puckers.

When stitching in straight lines, I tend to omit marking a

design. I let the side of the walking foot act as my guide. I move my needle to widen the channels. If I want to make the channels wider, I will use masking tape as my guide. The walking foot also comes with an arm that attaches and can be adjusted to accommodate your measurements. I even let seams be my guide sometimes. But I don't bother marking straight lines.

I recommend that you increase your stitch length a little when stitching with the even-feed foot. The added thickness from the batting warrants it. Make one stitch as you begin and pull the bobbin thread to the top. Holding the two threads out of the way, begin stitching.

With your hands, spread the quilt slightly around the needle. Keeping the quilt taut will also eliminate puckering. Begin stitching with shortened stitches and gradually increase them to the length of the normal stitching. Stitching in place will cause a knot to form on the bottom and the knot is undesirable. As you reach the end of your line of stitching, gradually reduce the length of the stitches again.

Hand placement for machine quilting

Pull the bobbin thread to the top once you have clipped the threads. With a large-eyed needle, thread the tails into the needle and then weave the needle between the top and backing in the batting. Bring the needle to the top surface again and clip the tails at the surface, burying the tails in the center of the quilt.

Your batting will dictate how much quilting and how far apart the lines of quilting can be. No matter what the packaging says, though, I recommend that the lines of quilting be no more than 2 1/2" or 3" apart. I think your quilt will look better. In addition, the amount of quilting should be evenly spaced across the entire surface of the quilt. Heavy quilting in the center and light quilting in the borders will cause the borders to ripple. Likewise, heavy quilting in the borders and light quilting in the center will cause center rippling. Even quilting lets your quilt lie or hang flat.

Tied Quilts

Sometimes you will find that the quilt cannot be quilted in the traditional manner. Because of the material used to make the quilt, such as denim, or the use of the quilt, such as a quickly made lap quilt, or because the batting you chose has a very high loft, you might find that tying the quilt is more beneficial than hand or machine quilting. Tying is a way of securing the three layers by evenly spaced knots over the surface of the quilt. Tying can be from the front or the back, depending on the look you desire. The distance between ties is dictated by the batting, so read the batting qualities and instructions carefully.

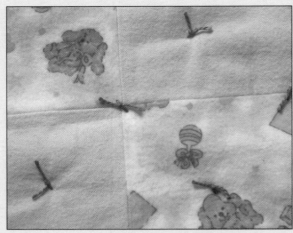
Tied quilt (Dorothy Kohout)

Thread

You may use a variety of threads to tie your quilt. In the past, our foremothers used everything from embroidery floss to knitting yarn. The trick is to choose something that will not loosen once it is tied. If you use the floss, plan to use all six plies. If you use a polyester knitting yarn, test to see if the knot will stay knotted. You might find that wool yarn will stay knotted better. A crochet thread might not stay knotted, either. Some threads can be pretty slick. The look that you are trying to achieve may also determine which thread you use.

Buttons

Using buttons to tie your quilt will add a wonderful embellishment. Combining an assortment of buttons with the knot will add charm and a wonderful folk quality.

Or, you might machine stitch, in place, a short length of

ribbon, tying each into a bow for an added touch of security and elegance.

Tied with buttons (Linda Mooney)

Decorative Machine Stitches

Another way to "tie" a quilt is to set your sewing machine with your favorite stitched motif. This can be a star, a flower or even a heart shape. By stitching the single motif, using the same spacing criteria of the knots and buttons mentioned previously, you can secure the

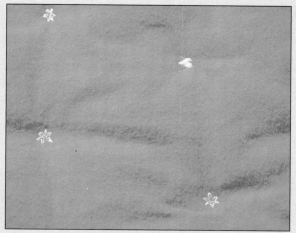

Machine stitched "ties" (Dorothy Kohout)

three layers, giving your quilt an entirely different look. Notice that the quilt that Dorothy Kohout made (pictured on this page), includes a variety of stitches, randomly spaced. Notice, too, that the spacing, while random, is still about a fist's distance in length.

The Knot

To tie a quilt, determine a grid. How far apart will the ties be? The batting will determine, but if in doubt, I recommend that the knots be no farther apart than the width of your fist, especially if the packaging says you can quilt as far apart as 9". Remember, lines of quilting provide more strength than a single knot every so often, so you will need to tie more densely than the maximum spacing that the batting allows.

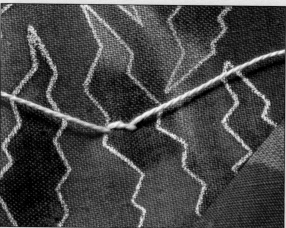

The tie

Begin with a long length of your thread and a sharp needle. Do not knot the end of the thread. Poke the threaded needle through all three layers of the quilt and come back up to the top about 1/8" from the first penetration, leaving about a 1 1/2" tail. Poke the needle back into the first hole and come up again in the second hole. The thread will have looped completely around the 1/8″ spot.

Without cutting the thread, go to the next spot, a fist's width away from the first, and poke the needle through to the back. Come up again 1/8″ away. Poke the needle back into the first hole and come up again in the second. Without cutting the thread, go to the next spot, a fist's width away from the second. Continue in this manner until you have covered your quilt with evenly spaced loops. Leave a 1 1/2″ tail on each of the last loops you make with each of your threads.

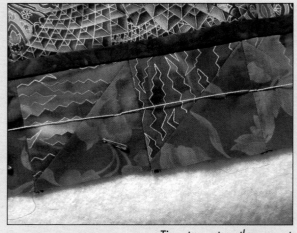

Ties strung together, uncut

Cut the thread between each spot. You will have 1 1/2″ tails at each point. Make a double knot at each spot. You may leave your tails the length they are or you may cut them to about 1/2″ in length.

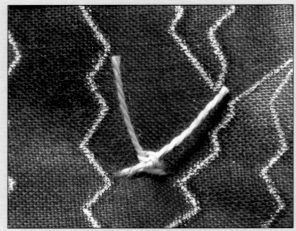

Tie, cut, knotted and trimmed

Binding

Depending on the batting you have chosen, or the *loft*, (the thickness), you will cut strips for your binding either 2 1/2″ wide or 2 1/4″ wide. To determine the number of strips you will need, measure the top and a side, multiply by two (to get the total circumference of your quilt top) and then divide by 40 (the average usable length of a strip cut selvage to selvage, after the selvage is removed). A partial strip should be counted as a whole strip. If the number you get is, say, 5.666, then you would cut 6 strips. If the number is 5.98, I cut 7 strips. I want the extra length.

To determine the amount of fabric needed for the binding, multiply the number of strips that are needed by 2 1/2″ and then round up about 1/8 yard. This gives you enough to straighten the fabric before you begin cutting the strips and even make a mistake. (I always multiply by 2 1/2″ even if I'm going to make the strips 2 1/4″ wide.) Say I need 6 strips. That's 15 inches. I'll round up to 1/2 yard (18″) and that will give me another strip should I need it. If I had needed exactly 18" I would still have rounded up so that I would have extra just in case.

Remove the selvages and sew the strips together on the bias across the tails, not through them.

Sewing the strips

Trim the excess so that you have a 1/4" seam allowance and press the seam open. This will help to eliminate bulk. Press the entire strip in half (the full length) wrong side in. Now you're ready to bind your quilt.

Seams pressed open and trimmed

Pressing the strips

I do not trim away the excess batting or backing before adding the binding. But I do make sure that the corners are square. Using your 12 1/2" square ruler, mark the corners square if they have been distorted at all. When sewing the binding to the quilt, let this line guide you in the corners, not the edge of the quilt top.

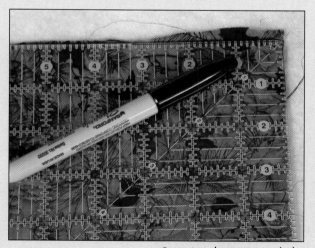

Squaring the corner w/ruler

Fit your sewing machine with your walking foot. Move your needle to the far right position so that it is 1/4" to

3/8" from the outside edge of the quilt top. The edge of the foot will be your sewing guide. At this point I have not removed any of the excess batting or backing. I wait to do that after the binding is attached. I also increase the length of my stitches just a bit since I'm going to be sewing through more thickness than when I piece.

Corner marked

Begin in the center of a side. Leaving a 10-12" tail, sew the binding, raw edges to the edge of your quilt top or the marking you made for the square corner. Sew to the corner but not all the way through the corner. Stop the same distance from the corner that your needle is from the edge of the quilt, 1/4" to 3/8". Pull the quilt out from under the needle and foot and turn the quilt so that you will be sewing the next edge. Fold the binding at a 45-degree angle from the stitched part. The raw edge of the binding and the raw edge of the quilt top will form a straight line. If not, it's probably because I stitched beyond where I should have. If that's the case, then I will clip that last stitch. This allows me to pull the binding back farther so that I do make that straight line. If it is straight, then fold the binding down over the corner, aligning the raw

edge with the new side. Begin sewing again from just off the edge to just before the next corner and repeat.

Sewing the binding

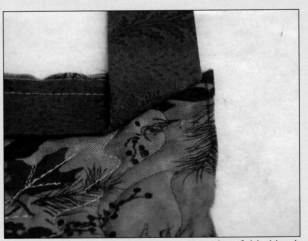

Binding folded back

When you get to the final side, stop sewing about 12-15" from where you began. At this point there are several ways to finish, some appearing bulkier than others. The method I use isn't really that hard once you get the hang of it, and it gives me a smooth join. So let me walk you through this slowly. Once you get it, you'll be delighted with the technique.

Bring the two tails together in the middle of the unsewn space. Fold the tails back on themselves so that there is about a 1/8" gap between the two where the folds meet. Make a small clip though all four layers of the binding fabric right where they meet in the center, perpendicular to the raw edge. Be sure that your clip is no deeper than about 1/8". You don't want to clip through where you will be sewing your seam.

Clipping the center points

The mitered corner

Now place your quilt on your table so that the edge on which you are working is right in front of you and the rest of the quilt is across the table. Open the left tail. The right side will be toward the quilt top and the wrong side will be showing. Place your left hand, palm up, on the quilt top behind the open binding (the binding is between you and your hand). With your right hand, flip the tail over, toward your hand, so that the wrong side of the binding is now in your hand and the right side is facing up. Angle the end of the tail toward the center of your quilt.

Open the right tail so that the wrong side is facing up

and angle it toward the center of the quilt top. Now place the right tail on top of the left tail. Cross them at a 45-degree angle to each other. Match the clips you made so that the correct placement occurs. Place a pin to hold the matched points in place. You will be sewing across the tails, so place your pins perpen-dicular to the sewing line.

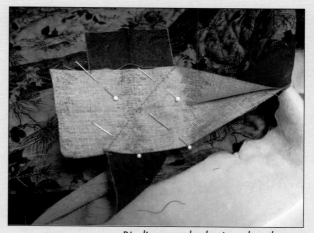

Binding matched, pinned and sewn

Press the seam open and trim for a 1/4" seam allowance. Fold the binding again as you had in the beginning and press the seam. Align the raw edges to your quilt top and finish sewing the binding to the top between the point where you began and ended. You should notice that the binding is flat and smooth!

Once the binding is attached you are ready to remove the excess batting and backing. I always want to be sure that the batting completely fills my binding. To that end I cut the excess, leaving about 1/8" extending past the raw edge of the binding.

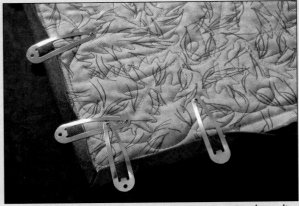
Binding clips

I suggest that you sew with a sharp or straw needle and match the thread to the binding fabric. Knot the end of a single strand of thread, remembering to knot the end you cut from the spool. (See page 64 for a review of threading the needle and the quilter's knot.) Hide the knot on the underside of the binding and sew the binding to the back of the quilt, hiding the machine stitches. Take a small stitch in the back, being careful not to go all the way through to the front, and then bring the needle through the edge of the binding, right in the fold. The stitch will be hidden in the fabric. The stitches should be short and close together so that the binding is secure.

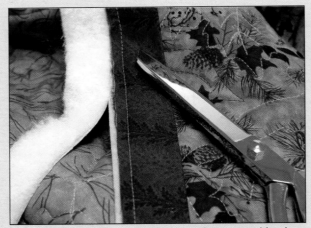
Trimming batting and backing

To complete the binding, fold the finished edge around the raw edge to the back, just covering the machine stitching. You won't have to pin all of the binding to the back, but you will find that securing some as you're working will keep the fabric from stretching. Some quilters will use pins, pinning in the direction they stitch so they don't prick knuckles. My favorite method uses "binding clips" that have, for a previous generation, acted as hair clips! You will find these marvelous tools at your local quilt shop.

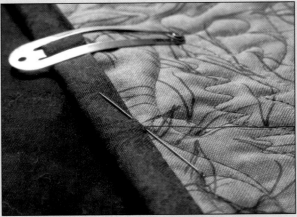
Stitching the binding

At the corners, clip the corner tips off (top, batting and batting, not binding), tuck the fold that is created by the mitered corner in the binding in the opposite direction of the fold on the front side. This will distribute the bulk so that the corner is smoother. If the binding gaps in the corner, stitch the fold. This will make an even neater corner.

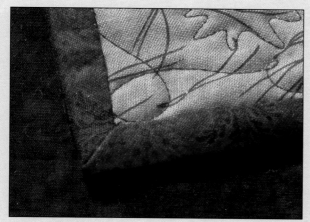

Corner

Documentation

Once the binding is completely sewn, you may think that you are finished with the quilt! But your next step is to document the quilt. Think of all the quilts that are passed from generation to generation with no documentation. That means we will never know who made the quilt, why she made the quilt and for whom. And we can only guess at how she made the quilt and with what. Are all those patches made from the clothing she made for her family over the years? Did she make the quilt to remember a special event? Did she make it for a cherished daughter who was leaving her home for a new life in the west? Unfortunately, we will never know.

Don't let future generations only wonder about your quilt. Document the quilt by adding a label to the back.

Labels

Your label can be elaborate or simple. You can draw pictures with a permanent marking pen on fabric or embroider a design. You may simply write with a permanent marker on a square of muslin or may print a label on your computer printer. Or you may even make an extra block from the front design to use as the label. Whatever you decide, make the label an important part of your quilt making.

Your label should include your name and the city in which you lived when you made the quilt. It should include the date you finished. You might even wish to include the date you began. If the quilt is a gift for someone special, you might even include the details of the occasion on the label. Some quilters are even including a photo transfer of themselves and the

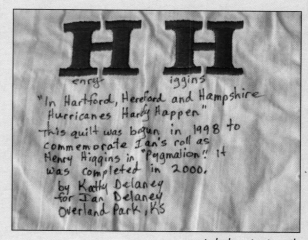

Label on Ian's quilt

recipient on the label. You might even consider including washing instructions on the label, especially if it is a gift for a non-quilter.

Once you have made the label, stitch it to the back of the quilt. Most quilters place it in the bottom right corner. But it's your quilt; place the label where you like!

Display

Not all quilts are put on a bed. Some are thrown across the back of a sofa, some are draped over a table and some are hung on the wall. Hanging the quilt on the wall requires something to hold the quilt suspended. The weight of the quilt will very rarely allow you to tack it up, and doing so would certainly cause damage to the wall and the quilt!

There are a variety of display mechanisms that you may employ. Your local quilt store may even have some examples. But the simplest way to display your quilt is to slip it over a rod that is attached to the wall, much the same way a simple curtain is hung in a window. If you slip it over a rod, though, you will need to attach a sleeve to the back of the quilt through which you will slide the rod.

Sleeve

The sleeve is the pocket through which the rod is placed and so must be large enough to accommodate it. Besides being large enough to enclose the rod, it must account for the fact that the rod is probably round. That means that you have to allow some "give." Otherwise

the quilt will fold around the rod instead of hanging straight.

I know that there are several ways to make a sleeve, but let me share with you the method I like to use. I know it will work for you!

To begin with, choose a fabric that is the same or very similar to the backing fabric if you can. It will give your quilt a more finished look.

Finished center seam and finished ends

Measure your quilt from side to side and subtract an inch. Cut a strip of fabric that width by 8 inches. If you don't have a single piece the correct length you can piece it, right sides together, using a 1/2" seam allowance. If you piece the strip, though, be sure to finish the seam. Trim one of the seam allowance layers to 1/4" and then fold the other layer over the first. Press the layers all to one side, enclosing the raw edges within. You will have 1/4" seam allowance with a finished edge. Machine stitch the seam allowance to the strip so that it will be flat to the wrong side of the fabric. You want to be sure that there are no gaps for the rod to hang up on when you are sliding it through.

Once you have your strip, finish the short ends. Fold the raw edge 1/4" and press, wrong sides together. Fold again and press. Machine stitch the hem to secure, again, taking care to leave no gaps on which the rod can catch. Repeat on the other short end.

Fold the strip in half lengthwise, wrong sides together, and sew 1/2" from the raw edge, forming a tube. Press the tube flat. Fold the seam allowance on the stitching line and press. This is the back of the sleeve.

1st pressing

With the back of the sleeve facing down on your ironing board, raise the front layer of the sleeve up and create a second crease 1 1/2" from the crease that's already there from your first pressing. Press the new crease without touching the first crease. This second crease is the bottom edge that you will stitch to the back of your quilt.

Measure 1 1/2" below the top binding of your quilt on the back. Pin the edge of the sleeve with the seam allowance along this line, centering the sleeve between the sides of the quilt.

(I fold the sleeve in half and note the middle. Then I fold the quilt in half and match the middle to the center of the sleeve.) Pin the second crease that you created so that the back of the sleeve is flat against the quilt. Note that the front side of the sleeve is not flat to the quilt but acts as a pleat.

Second crease

Stitch the sleeve back to the quilt back on all four edges. Be sure to pin in the direction that you stitch so that the pins don't hurt your knuckles.

Completed sleeve

CHAPTER 6
THE PROJECTS

"4-PATCH STRIP"
54 1/2" x 67"
by Kathy Delaney, Overland Park, KS, quilted by Kelly Ashton, 2003

4-PATCH STRIP
55 1/2" x 69"

Fabrics required:

- 1/8 yard from 7 fabrics for 4-patch blocks

- 2 yards for alternate blocks and strips

- 1/2 yard for inner border (will be pieced)

- 2 yards for outer border (I used the same fabric as strips.)

- 3 5/8 yards for backing

- 1/2 yard for binding

- 60" x 74" piece of batting

Constructing the Blocks

For a review of the 4-Patch block, see page 28.

Cutting instructions:

From each of the 1/8-yard strips, cut a 3 1/2" strip. Cut a total of (72) 3 1/2" x 3 1/2" squares from the 3 1/2" strips (about 9-11 from each fabric for a total of 72).

From the length of the alternate block fabric, cut (3) strips 6" x about 56". (Note that these are different than the blocks. You will use a 6" x 24" rotary cutting ruler for simplicity.) Set these aside for now. From the remainder, cut (18) 6 1/2" x 6 1/2" squares.

Piecing Instructions:

With right sides together, pair two 3 1/2" x 3 1/2" squares from different prints and stitch 1/4" from one edge.

String piecing

To save thread, string-piece the pairs until you have stitched 36 pairs. That is, piece one pair right after the other without cutting your thread between pairs. (All 36 pairs will be strung together like the flag streamers at a used car lot.) You will have (36) 3 1/2" x 6 1/2" units.

Clip the units apart with your thread snips and press the seam allowances in one direction. (Press, don't iron!)

With right sides together, pair two units together. The seam allowances should be opposing and snug together. Again, string-piece the pairs with a 1/4" seam allowance until you have stitched 18 blocks.

Clip the blocks apart. Before pressing any of the seam allowances, turn one of the blocks over and notice that the pressed seam allowances are in opposite directions. You are going to press the new seam in opposite directions, splitting the seam in the center at the intersection. For a review of the "twist" see page 31. Your 4-Patch blocks should measure 6 1/2" x 6 1/2".

Putting it all Together

This quilt is made up of a total of seven vertical rows. Four of the rows are pieced and the other three are solid strips of fabric.

Let's begin by piecing the four rows. Two of the rows will begin and end with a 4-Patch block; you will need (5) 4-Patch blocks and (4) 6 1/2" x 6 1/2" squares. Two of the rows will begin and end with a plain square; you will need (5) 6 1/2" x 6 1/2" squares and (4) 4-Patch blocks. The two different rows will look like the diagrams below.

Press the seam allowances all toward the plain block.

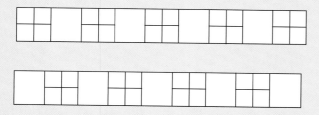

Once you have the four pieced rows sewn you will be ready to sew them, along with the previously cut strips into your quilt top. Begin by measuring your pieced strips. If you have used a consistent 1/4" seam allowance, your strips should measure 54 1/2" long. If you didn't sew with an exact 1/4" seam allowance but were consistent with the one you used, each of the strips should be the same length. That is the length to which you need to trim the 6" strips. Take a look at the picture of the quilt top and notice that you begin and end with a pieced strip. Sew the strips together to complete the center of your quilt top.

Now you are ready to add the borders. The border design for this quilt is called long horizontal. This means that the top and bottom, the horizontal borders, are the longest border strips.

Measure through the center of your top vertically. Divide that measurement by 40" and you will have the number of 2 1/2" strips that you will need to cut from your inner border fabric for one side of the quilt top. Cut enough for two. Remove the selvage from the strips and piece the strips together until you have two strips that are 2 1/2" by the length of your quilt top. Sew

the strips to either side of your quilt top. Press the seam allowance to the border.

Measure through the center of your top horizontally. Divide that measurement by 40" and you will have the number of 2 1/2" strips that you will need to cut from your inner border fabric for the top or bottom of your quilt top. Cut enough for two. Remove the selvage from the strips and piece the strips together until you have two strips that are 2 1/2" by the width of your quilt top. Sew the strips to the top and bottom of your quilt top. Press the seam allowance to the border.

Measure again as you did for the inner border. From the outer border fabric, cut (4) 6" strips the length of the measurement you just calculated. Repeat the steps you followed for the inner border. The only difference is that you will not first piece the strips. You will just trim the length of the strip according to your measurements. Sew the side strips on first and then the top and bottom. Again, press the seam allowance to the border.

Finishing

Baste your quilt top with the backing and batting in the method of your choice, thread or pins. Quilt by hand or machine and then add the binding. For a review, begin reading on page 81.

And now, use your imagination and have some fun! Quilt as desired and bind your quilt to finish. Don't forget the label!

"HOURGLASS TABLE RUNNER #1"
19 3/4" x 42 3/4"
by Kathy Delaney, Overland Park, KS, 2004

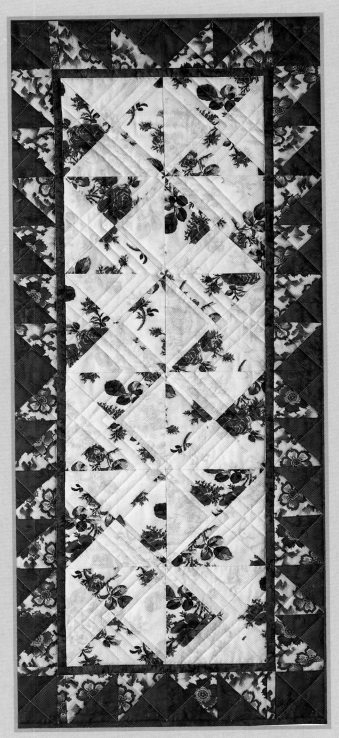

"HOURGLASS TABLE RUNNER #2"
19 1/2" x 42 3/4"
by Kathy Delaney, Overland Park, KS, 2004

HOURGLASS TABLE RUNNER
19 1/2" x 43"

Fabric requirements:

• 1/2 yard each of two coordinating fabrics
(I used a floral and a geometric with the same colors.)
for the center Hourglass Pinwheel blocks

• 1/4 yard each of two contrasting fabrics that pick
up the colors from the center blocks
(I used a coordinating print with the same colors and a
strong tone on tone of one of the colors in the prints.)
for the half-square triangle units in the outer border

• 1/8 yard of a strong contrasting fabric
for the inner border

• 1 1/4 yard for backing

• 1/3 yard for binding
(I used the same fabric as my tone-on-tone
in the outer border.)

• 24" x 47" batting
(You might consider using a very thin batting since this is
for a table top and may have something sitting on it.)

Making the Blocks

For a review of the Hourglass Pinwheel block, see page 47.

From the two coordinating fabrics you chose for the Hourglass blocks, cut (2) 7 1/2" strips each from selvage to selvage. Subcut the strips into (6) 7 1/2" x 7 1/2" squares from each fabric. Pair the squares, one from each fabric, for a total of six pairs.

With right sides together, draw a diagonal line on the wrong side of the lighter fabric. Sew 1/4" from the line, on both sides of the line. Cut on the line, dividing the fabric into two half-square triangle units. Press the seam allowance to the darker of the two fabrics. Pair the units, right sides together, so that one is on top of the other and the fabrics alternate.

With right sides together, and the fabrics alternating, the seams should snug together with the seam allowances pressed in opposite directions. Draw a diagonal line through the seam and sew 1/4" from the line, on both sides of the line, and cut on the line, dividing the units into two hourglass blocks. You should have 12 hourglass units.

Arrange four hourglass units into a 4-Patch. Be sure to turn the units a quarter turn each time so that the fabrics alternate. Sew the 4-Patch blocks, making a total of three Hourglass Pinwheel blocks. Sew the three blocks together, again, rotating the blocks to alternate fabrics, to complete the center of your table runner.

First Border

From the 1/8 yard cut (3) 1" strips, selvage to selvage. Measure the longest length of the table runner center and trim two of the strips to that measurement. Sew the strips to the long sides of the table runner center. Press the seam allowances to the strips.

Measure the width of the table runner center and trim the third strip, making two strips that measurement. Sew the strips to the short sides of the table runner center. Press the seam allowances to the strips.

Second Border

From the two outer border fabrics, cut (16) 4" x 4" squares. Pair the squares, one each from the two fabrics, right sides together. On the wrong side of the lighter of the two fabrics, draw a diagonal line. Sew 1/4" from the line, on both sides of the line. Cut through the sewn squares on the line and press the blocks open, pressing the seam allowance to the darker fabric.

Trim each of the half-square units to 3 1/2" x 3 1/2." You should have a total of 32 half-square units.

From the print fabric you used in the half-square triangle units, cut (8) 1" x 3 1/2" rectangles. From the tone-on-tone fabric you used in the half-square triangle units, cut (4) 3 1/2" x 3 1/2" squares.

Referring to the picture of the finished table runner,

arrange two sets of four half-square triangle units for the short ends and sew the units together. To the ends of each of the sets, sew a 1" x 3 1/2" rectangle, pressing the seam allowance to the triangle. Again, to the ends of the sets sew a 3 1/2" x 3 1/2" square of the tone-on-tone fabric, pressing the seam allowance to the square.

Again, referring to the picture of the finished table runner, arrange two sets of 12 half-square triangle units for the long edges and sew the units together. To the ends of each of the sets, sew a 1" x 3 1/2" rectangle.

Sew the long sets to the long edges of the table runner. Press the seam allowance to the first border strip. Sew the short sets to the short ends of the table runner. Press the seam allowance to the first border strip.

Refer to pages 85 to review basting and quilting and to page 96 for binding your table runner. I let the squares running down the very center of the table runner inspire my quilting designs. Let your imagination run wild and *quilt as desired,* finishing with a label.

"BIRDS IN THE AIR"

54 1/2" x 69"

by Kathy Delaney, Overland Park, KS, quilted by Martha Heimbaugh, 2003

BIRDS IN THE AIR
54" x 72"

Fabric requirements:

• (12) fat quarters for triangles
(You might consider mixing medium prints with smaller prints and stripes.)

• 2 yards for background

• 2 yards for border

• 1/2 yard for binding

• 3 1/2 yards for backing

• 62" x 80" piece of batting

Making the Blocks

Cutting Instructions - accuracy is very important to this project. Unless noted, all strips are cut across the grain of your fabric, from selvage to selvage.

For this quilt you will make a total of 59 Birds in the Air blocks. You will cut enough squares and triangles for 60 blocks, so you'll have one extra block.

Adjacent to the long edge of each of the fat quarters, cut (2) or (3) 6 7/8" x 6 7/8" squares, for a total of (30) squares. You will cut (2) squares each from all (12) of your fat quarters. Choose (6) of the fat quarters and cut (1) more square from each until you have cut the (30) that you need. Cut each of the squares once diagonally. You will have (60) 6 7/8" half-square triangles. Set these aside for now.

From your background fabric, cut (4) 2 7/8" strips. Cut each of these strips into (13) 2 7/8" x 2 7/8" squares (you may actually be able to cut 14 squares, depending on the width of your fabric). You need to have a total of (45) 2 7/8" x 2 7/8" squares. Cut each of the squares diagonally once, just as you cut the 6 7/8" x 6 7/8" squares. Set these aside for now.

As an alternative to the methods described beginning on page 38 for making 1/2-square triangle units, I'd like to introduce you to the grid papers I mentioned on page 39. They are such a time saver! You will need the preprinted paper that results in 2" finished 1/2-square triangle units. The grid paper we'll use comes on a roll so no folds

appear in the paper.

Begin by cutting a group of six units (squares) off of the roll. Make sure you have six complete units. (Each of the units will result in (2) 1/2-square triangle units. Cut directly on a solid line that extends across the width of the paper to separate the six from the rest of the roll. You will need (15) pieces of the triangle paper. For each piece of triangle paper you will need two pieces of fabric, 6" x 9", one from one of your fat quarters and one from your background fabric. In other words, you will need (1) 6" x 9" rectangle from each of your fat quarters and one more from three of the fat quarters for a total of fifteen.

With right sides together, pair a print with a background rectangle. On top of that, center and pin a triangle paper segment. Be sure that your pins do not cross any of the dotted lines printed on the paper.

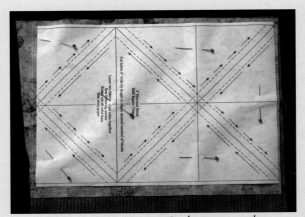

Grid papers ready to sew

With your sewing machine set on a straight stitch, sew on all of the dotted lines, following the arrows. Repeat with each of the remaining pairs or rectangles.

Use your rotary cutter and rotary cutting ruler to trim the paper segment on the solid lines on the outside edges. Accuracy in cutting will result in more accurate squares. Once trimmed, you can cut the squares apart, again, on the solid lines.

The directions that come with the paper will tell you to also cut on the diagonal lines. I find it easier to leave the diagonal lines intact for the next step. You can try both methods and see what works for you.

Removing the paper

Fold a triangle side of the paper over the stitching and then tear the paper away. Repeat on the other side. Give the square a little tug across the middle, holding the square on either side of the paper that remains. This will release the center strip of paper, which is then easily removed. You might notice that at this point your squares look just like they did when you made your 1/2-square triangle blocks for your Sampler quilt.

With small scissors, cut a notch out of the corners between the stitching. This will remove the extra triangle from the 1/2-square triangle units. Cut the blocks through the center channel between the stitching to separate the two 1/2-square triangle units. Press the squares open, pressing to the darker fabric, taking extra care that you don't distort the squares. You will have (180) 2 1/2" x 2 1/2" half-square triangle units.

Constructing the Block

Each square block is made up of two triangles; one is a pieced triangle and one is the 6 7/8" 1/2-square

Cutting the notch

triangle from the fat quarter prints. We will begin by making the pieced 1/2-square triangles.

For each block, you will need (3) 1/2-square triangle units, all from the same print, and (3) background triangles. Arrange them on your sewing table in front of you as shown in the photo.

Sew the two background triangles to the 1/2-square triangle unit as shown on the left of the photograph, being

Piecing diagram

very careful to maintain a consistent scant 1/4" seam allowance.

Sew the two 1/2-square triangle units together as shown on the right of the photograph and add the background triangle. Press the seam allowance toward the background fabric taking great care to avoid touching the bias edge of the triangles with the iron. Ironing the bias edge will cause the bias edge to stretch and distort. (The arrows in the photograph show you the pressing direction.) Sew the two new units together to form half of your block. Press the seam allowance toward the single 1/2-square triangle unit that you pieced together (on the left of the photograph), again taking great care not to touch the bias edge with the iron. This will let you see the crossing lines as you sew the two halves of the block together in the next step. You will need 59 of these pieced triangles though you have enough cut to make 60.

To complete the block, match a 6 7/8" 1/2-square triangle with a pieced triangle. For a scrappy look, mix the prints so that the prints of the two halves are not the same. With the pieced triangle on top, sew the two triangles together along the long edge, being careful to sew through the crossed seams. This will ensure that you won't cut off your points on the right side. The edge that you will be sewing will be a bias edge. This means that it will stretch easily. Eliminate stretching by guiding the fabric under the presser foot of your machine very gingerly, making every effort not to pull, thereby stretching.

Your block should look like the photograph. Press the seam to the large triangle being careful not to stretch the block. Your blocks should measure 6 1/2" x 6 1/2".

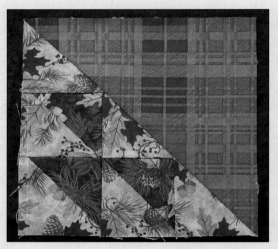

Birds in the Air block

PUTTING IT ALL TOGETHER

The Setting Triangles

From your background fabric, cut (2) 10" strips. From these strips, cut (5) 10" x 10" squares and (2) 7 1/2" x 7 1/2" squares. Cut the 7 1/2" x 7 1/2" squares diagonally once as you did your 6 7/8" x 6 7/8" squares. You will have (4) 1/2-square triangles. Cut the (5) 10" squares diago-nally twice. This will give you (4) 1/4-square triangles from each square, for a total of (20) 1/4-square triangles. These are the setting triangles.

Arrange your blocks in a pleasing manner, *on point*, in rows of five across and seven down. (On point means that the blocks are twisted so that they appear to be resting on a corner instead of a side.) The solid half of the block is above the pieced half of the block. A design wall would come in very handy here so that you can stand back and admire your arrangement, but laying them out on the floor would work, too. Some quilters find it helpful to stand on a ladder so that they can get a better view of the arrangement when it is on the floor.

Place the 1/4-square triangles around the edge of the arrangement, between the blocks. The longer edge of the triangle is the outside edge. The shorter edges will be sewn to the blocks. Place the 1/2-square triangles in the four corners. This time the longer edge will be sewn to the block.

You will sew the quilt top together in diagonal rows, the first row being the upper left corner, consisting of three setting triangles (one 1/2-square triangle and two 1/4-square triangles) and one block. Your second row will consist of two setting triangles (both 1/4-square triangles) and 3 blocks. Continue in this manner until your reach your last row, which is the same as the first, except the 1/2-square triangle is sewn to the opposite side.

Finishing

Baste your quilt top with the backing and batting in the method of your choice, thread or pins. Quilt by hand or machine and then add the binding. Don't forget that label!

"DOIN' THE
SAWTOOTH STRIP"
73" x 85"
by Kathy Delaney, Overland Park, KS,
quilted by Freda Smith, 2000

DOIN' THE SAWTOOTH STRIP
77" x 92"

Fabric Requirements:

- 2 yards for setting triangles
(This is the fabric that surrounds the stars, placing them on point.)

- 1 1/4 yards for star background

- 1/2 yard for star center

- 5/8 yard for star-points

- 1/3 yard for sashing

- 3 yards for border

- 3/4 yard for binding

- 5 1/2 yards for backing (42" wide)

- 81" x 96" piece of batting

Cutting Instructions:

(Unless otherwise noted, all cuts are from selvage to selvage, across the width of the fabric.) Refer to page 54 to review constructing a Sawtooth Star.

From setting triangle fabric, cut (3) strips, 19" each. Subcut the strips into a total of (5) 19" squares. Cut the 19" squares in half diagonally twice (once, in both directions), giving you (20) 1/4-square triangles (you need a total of 18 of them). After cutting your (5) 19" squares, you will have a piece left over from the third 19" strip; from this piece, cut (2) 11" x 11" squares. From the remainder of the setting triangle fabric, cut (1) 11" strip. Subcut the strip into (4) 11" x 11" squares. Now you should have a total of (6) 11-inch squares. Cut these in half diagonally once, giving you (12) 1/2-square triangles. Set these aside for now.

From the star background fabric, cut (5) strips 3 1/2" wide each. Subcut the strips into (48) 3 1/2" x 3 1/2" squares.

From the star background fabric, cut (2) strips 7 1/4 inches wide each. Subcut the strips into (12) 7 1/4" x 7 1/4" squares.

From the star-points fabric, cut (5) strips 3 7/8" wide each. Subcut the strips into (48) 3 7/8" x 3 7/8" squares.

(Please note that the preceding directions for cutting the background squares and the star points squares are for the Fast Flying Geese units that will make the Sawtooth Star blocks. Refer to page 50 to review Fast Flying Geese. While making your Sampler quilt you learned several different methods for making these units. Please review the various methods and feel free to use the method you like the best!)

From the star center fabric, cut (2) strips 6 1/2" wide each. Subcut the strips into (12) 6 1/2" x 6 1/2" squares.

Sawtooth Star block

From the sashing fabric, cut (4) strips 2 1/2" wide each. Remove the selvages and then sew 2 strips, end-to-end, creating a 2 1/2" x 80" sashing strip. Repeat with the other 2 strips.

Constructing the blocks:

This quilt consists of (12) 12" Sawtooth Star blocks set on point into strips. The setting triangles provide the sides of the strips. Three rows of four blocks are set with two sashing strips and then bordered with mitered corners.

Arrange the background squares, flying geese units and center block and sew the seams in the order you followed when making this block for your Sampler quilt. Refer to page 54 if you need to review. You will make 12 blocks.

Once you have constructed the 12 blocks, you will put them together in rows with the background setting triangles. The half-square triangles go at the ends of the strips while the quarter-square triangles go between the blocks. Refer to the photograph of the quilt on page 118. Note that the setting triangles are over-sized. This gives you the option of "floating" the Sawtooth Stars as in the sample quilt. If you choose not to float the stars, trim the edges 1/4' from the corner points of sawtooth star blocks. Your quilt's over-all dimensions will be smaller than the sample quilt.

Sew the three rows of Sawtooth Stars to the two sashing strips.

Adding the borders:

When I made this quilt I used a fabric that had a stripe design. Therefore, I made a mitered border. You may use the border style of your choice, depending on the fabric you chose. Refer to the instructions for a mitered corner, beginning on page 80.

Now you're ready to sandwich and baste the quilt top and do some fancy quilting in all those spaces afforded by the setting triangles! And, of course, document your quilt with a label.

By the way, if you use a stencil for your quilting design, you will notice little jumps in the design. These are bridges that hold the stencil in one piece. As you quilt, be sure to stitch right through those bridge spaces. Don't skip them.

"FENCED POSIES"
33" x 33"
by Kathy Delaney, Overland Park, KS,
quilted by Charlotte Gurwell, 2001

FENCED POSIES
35" x 35"

Fabric requirements:

- 1/2 yard Flower Block background

Flower appliqué

- 1/8 yard for flowers

- 1/8 yard for leaves

- 1/4 yard for sashing

Fence Border

- 1 1/8 yard for fence (a stripe will really enhance the fence)

- 3/4 yard for background

- 1 1/8 yard for backing

- 39" x 39" square of batting

- 1/3 yard for binding

You will also need:

- 1/2 yard light-weight paper-backed fusible web for the appliqué

- 1/2 yard stabilizer

- Black thread to outline the appliqué

Getting Started - Cutting the Fabric

Unless otherwise noted, all cuts are across the grain, from selvage to selvage. While your fabric may be 45" wide, as a rule of thumb, I am considering that you will have 40" of usable fabric.

Flower Block background

While these blocks will finish out at 6 inches, you will need them to be larger as you begin. Start by cutting (9) 7" x 7" squares or larger. After you complete the appliqué, you will trim the blocks to 6 1/2" x 6 1/2" square before piecing the top.

Fence Border blocks

Most stripes run the length of the fabric instead of across (selvage to selvage), you will need to cut strips from the length. You may have to cut extra, make an extra strip set, in order to get the number of subcuts that are required. I have allowed extra fabric in your amounts to accommodate this eventuality. Cutting accurately, and sewing an accurate 1/4" seam allowance, is important so that the points match where you need them to match.

From the fence stripe fabric, rotary cut (6) 1 1/2" strips. These must be cut from the length of the fabric to accommodate the stripe print. Be sure to cut these first before you cut anything else. Remove the selvage edges before cutting your strips.

From the fence stripe fabric, rotary cut (2) 6 1/2" strips. These are cut from the remainder of the striped fabric and are cut across the grain instead of the length. Subcut the 6 1/2" strips into (20) 2 1/2" x 6 1/2" rectangles.

From the background fabric, cutting across the grain, selvage to selvage, cut (8) 1 1/2" strips and (3) 2 1/2" strips. From two of the 1 1/2" strips, cut (40) 1 1/2" x 1 1/2" squares.

From the sashing fabric, cutting across the grain, from selvage to selvage, cut (2) 2 1/2" strips. Subcut each strip into (1) 22 1/2" x 2 1/2" and (3) 6 1/2" x 2 1/2" strips.

Preparing Your Appliqué Blocks

The sample quilt on page 122 is machine appliquéd so I used fusible web to iron onto my appliqué. Follow the directions that came with the fusible product that you are using. I recommend that you use a lightweight fusible. You may choose, instead, to hand appliqué. Whatever method is your favorite, use the templates provided. I used a plastic template material to make just one template of each shape and I used that template to trace onto the paper side of my fusible material. Note that the leaves are mirror images from left to right. By adjusting where you place the leaves behind the posy you will get the different shapes for the bottom leaves. To review appliqué, refer to page 67 for hand appliqué and page 72 for machine appliqué.

My machine has a buttonhole stitch that replicates the hand buttonhole stitch. You may choose to use a satin stitch or a zig zag stitch. Either way, you will want to sew a decorative stitch around each element of your appliqué, to secure the appliqué to the background and to finish the raw edges.

After you have finished the appliqué, press from the wrong side and then trim your blocks, centering the posy, to 6 1/2" x 6 1/2" square.

To six of the trimmed blocks, sew a 2 1/2" x 6 1/2" sashing strip to the right side of the block. Sew the six blocks together in pairs, keeping the sashing to the right side. Add the three remaining blocks to the right edge of each of the pairs. You should have three rows of posies with sashing between.

Measure the length of the rows. If your seam allowances are a consistent 1/4", the rows will probably measure 22 1/2" long. To the bottom of two of the rows, sew the 2 1/2" x 22 1/2" sashing strips. Sew these two units together, keeping the long sashing strips to the bottom. Add the remaining row to the bottom of the second row. You now have the center for your quilt finished.

POSY BLOCKS

1 2

6

5

3 4

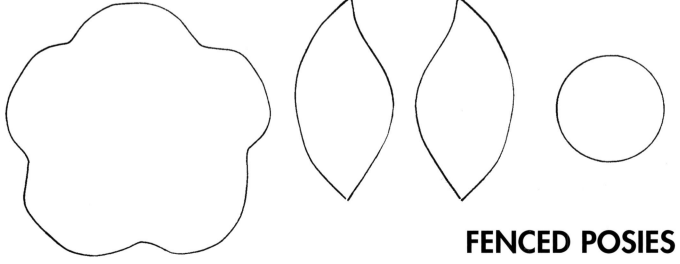

FENCED POSIES

Preparing the Fence Border

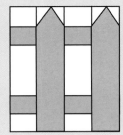

This is Fence Block A. It will finish to measure 6 1/2" x 8 1/2" (6" x 8" finished). You will need to make eight for this wall hanging.

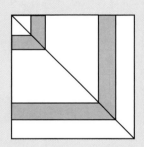

This is Fence Block B. It will finish to measure 6 1/2" x 6 1/2" (6" x 6" finished). You will need to make four for this wall hanging.

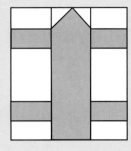

This is the Corner Block. It will finish to measure 6 1/2" x 6 1/2" (6" x 6" finished). You will need to make (4) for this wall hanging.

Begin by making three strip sets. The grey in the drawing below represents the 1 1/2" strips of your fence stripe fabric. The white is the background: (2) 1 1/2" strips and (1) 2 1/2" strip.

I pressed my seams to the stripe so that it would appear as though my fence is forward to my background.

Subcut the strip sets into (24) 2 1/2" rectangles and (8) 6 1/2" squares (these are the "rails"). Set these aside until you get your pickets made.

For each of the (20) pickets, you will need (1) 2 1/2" x 6 1/2" rectangle of fence stripe and (2) 1 1/2" square of background.

Place a background square on a stripe rectangle, right sides together, as shown below. Sew as shown by the dotted line.

Fold the square back, along the stitching line, to the outer corner and press. Trim out the center layer of fabric. DO NOT cut away the fence stripe.

Repeat, as shown in the next diagram, with the second square of background fabric.

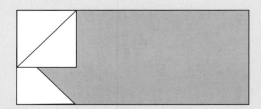

Again, press the square along the stitching toward the outside corner. Trim away the center layer, leaving the fence stripe intact. You will need to make (20) pickets in this manner.

Block A

To each picket, sew a rail onto the left side of the picket, pressing to the picket. You will want to pay extra attention to matching the point where the rail meets the side point of the picket. You should have (20) picket-rail units. Sew (2) picket-rail units together to make a Block A. You need (8) of Block A.

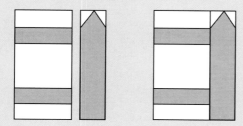

Block B

To the (4) remaining picket-rail units, sew a rail to the right side. You will have (4) of Block B.

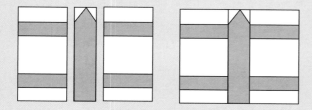

For each side of the quilt, sew two Blocks A together and add a Block B to the right side. The entire fence unit should begin and end with a rail. Now you are ready to make the four corner blocks.

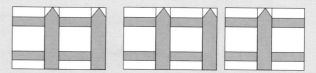

From your strip sets, you should have cut (8) 6 1/2" x 6 1/2" squares. With right sides together, and with the stripes going in the same direction and exactly matching, draw a line on the wrong side, diagonally from corner to corner. This is your stitching line. Trim (as shown by the solid line). Press the seam open. You will have four Corner Blocks.

To the ends of (2) of the fence units, add the corner blocks. Make sure that the rails turn "up" so as to go around the corner. Now you're ready to finish the quilt!

Putting It All Together

To the quilt center, sew the two fence units (without the corner blocks) to either side, making sure that the pickets point inward. Press to the Posy Blocks.

To the top and bottom, sew the two fence units (with the corner blocks), making sure that the pickets point inward. Press to the Posy Blocks.

At this point you are ready to add the backing, batting and quilt. Follow with the binding and you are finished with your wall quilt! Have I mentioned putting on a label?

"RAIL FENCE A BLOOMIN' "
40" x 50"
by Kathy Delaney, Overland Park, KS, quilted by Martha Heimbaugh, 2004

RAIL FENCE A BLOOMIN'
40" x 50" crib quilt

Fabric requirements:

- 3/8 yard pale yellow for Rail Fence blocks

- 3/8 yard pale yellow and blue mixed print for Rail Fence blocks

- 3/8 yard pale blue for Rail Fence blocks

- 3/8 yard medium yellow for inside border and flower centers

- 1/4 yard for outside border

- (1) fat quarter dark blue for appliqué stems

- 1/8 yard medium blue for appliqué leaves

- 1/8 yard each of 5 blues (medium to dark) for flowers

- 3/8 yard for binding

- 1 1/2 yards of 45" wide fabric for backing

- 44" x 54" piece of batting

CUTTING INSTRUCTIONS

Begin by making the Rail Fence blocks. You will make a total of six blocks. Cut (4) 2 1/2" wide strips from each of the three Rail Fence fabrics, from the width of the fabric, selvage to selvage.

Cut (4) 2 1/2" wide strips from the inner border fabric. Cut (4) 6 1/2" wide strips from the outer border fabric.

PUTTING IT TOGETHER

For a review of the Rail Fence block, see page 31. Arrange the strips you cut for the Rail Fence in the order you wish them to appear in the block. I put a yellow fabric and a blue fabric on either side of the yellow/blue print. Press very carefully so that you don't stretch your strip sets. For a review of pressing, see page 24. Your strip sets should measure 6 1/2" wide.

Using a 6 1/2" x 6 1/2" square rotary cutting ruler, cut the strip sets into a total of (24) 6 1/2" x 6 1/2" squares. Lay the squares out on a table, design wall or your floor and play with them. The Rail Fence block that you made for the Sampler quilt is not the only way. You can arrange the squares so that the strips stair-step diagonally across the quilt top as on the Rail Fence quilt in the gallery on page 148. Or you can arrange them as you did for your sampler, deciding which fabric that you want to spoke from the center. Each choice is valid.

Once you have decided on an arrangement, sew the blocks together, as a 4-patch, twisting the center. For a review of twisting the center, see page 31. You will make six blocks. Sew the blocks together into three rows, each with two blocks.

Measure through the center of the quilt top, vertically. Cut two of your inner border strips to match this measurement and sew to the sides of the quilt top. Press the seam allow-ances to the strips.

Measure through the center of your quilt top, horizontally, and cut the remaining two inner border strips to match this measurement. Sew the strips to the top and bottom of the quilt top, pressing the seam allowances to the strips.

The outer border style on this quilt uses a block at each of the corners. This is an excellent border to use when you don't have quite enough fabric for the full length. This style also adds an extra design element, as I have done here. It serves to stop the appliqué so that you don't have to worry about the vine meeting perfectly at the corners. While making the design continue to the corner would have been easy enough, I thought you might like the freedom that the corners allow when designing your vine.

Decide if you want to hand or machine appliqué the designs onto your borders. For machine appliqué, review, beginning on page 72. For appliqué by hand, review, beginning on page 67.

Measure through the center of the quilt top again, both vertically and horizontally, to determine the length of the side, top and bottom appliqué border strips. I recommend that you add an inch or two to the length so that any distortion caused by your appliqué stitches doesn't make the strips end up being too short. I also recommend making the ends of the vines a little longer, too. You will also need (4) 6 1/2" x 6 1/2" squares for the corners. Cut your background squares 7 1/2" x 7 1/2" before you appliqué the design and trim to 6 1/2" square when you've finished.

Using the method of your choosing, appliqué the vine with posies to the border strips and the posy with leaves to the squares, following the patterns begining on page 132, aligning the center markings. Note that the templates for the border are the same templates used for the "Fenced Posies" quilt, beginning on page 122. I used the plastic templates that I had made for that quilt to trace my freezer paper templates, using the pattern guides, beginning on page 132 for placement and stitched the appliqué by hand. The vines can be made using several methods. I used a tool I found in my local quilt shop called a Bias Tape Maker to make my bias vines before appliquéing them to the background. I used the 3/8" size.

You may also make templates for the vine segments and employ needle turn appliqué to attach them to the background.

When you have completed the appliqué, press the strips from the wrong side and trim according to the measurements of your quilt top. Sew the side borders to the quilt top with a 1/4" seam allowance and press to the strip.

Sew two appliquéd squares to the ends of the top and bottom strips, pressing the seam allowances to the strips. When you sew the top, bottom and side border strips to the quilt top you will find that the seams snug together at the corners.

Now you are ready to baste your quilt sandwich and *quilt as desired*! Notice that the vine in the borders seems to frame the center of the quilt top. The quilting on my quilt lets that vine act as a separation between the center of the quilt top and the outside edge. Don't forget the label!

The patterns for the border applique are on the following pages. The dotted lines indicate that the pattern overlaps the next segment. "A" is followed by "B" and "B" is followed by "C" and so on.

APPLIQUÉ TEMPLATES:

Top and Bottom Borders
A
outside edge
1
9
7
8
10
2
11

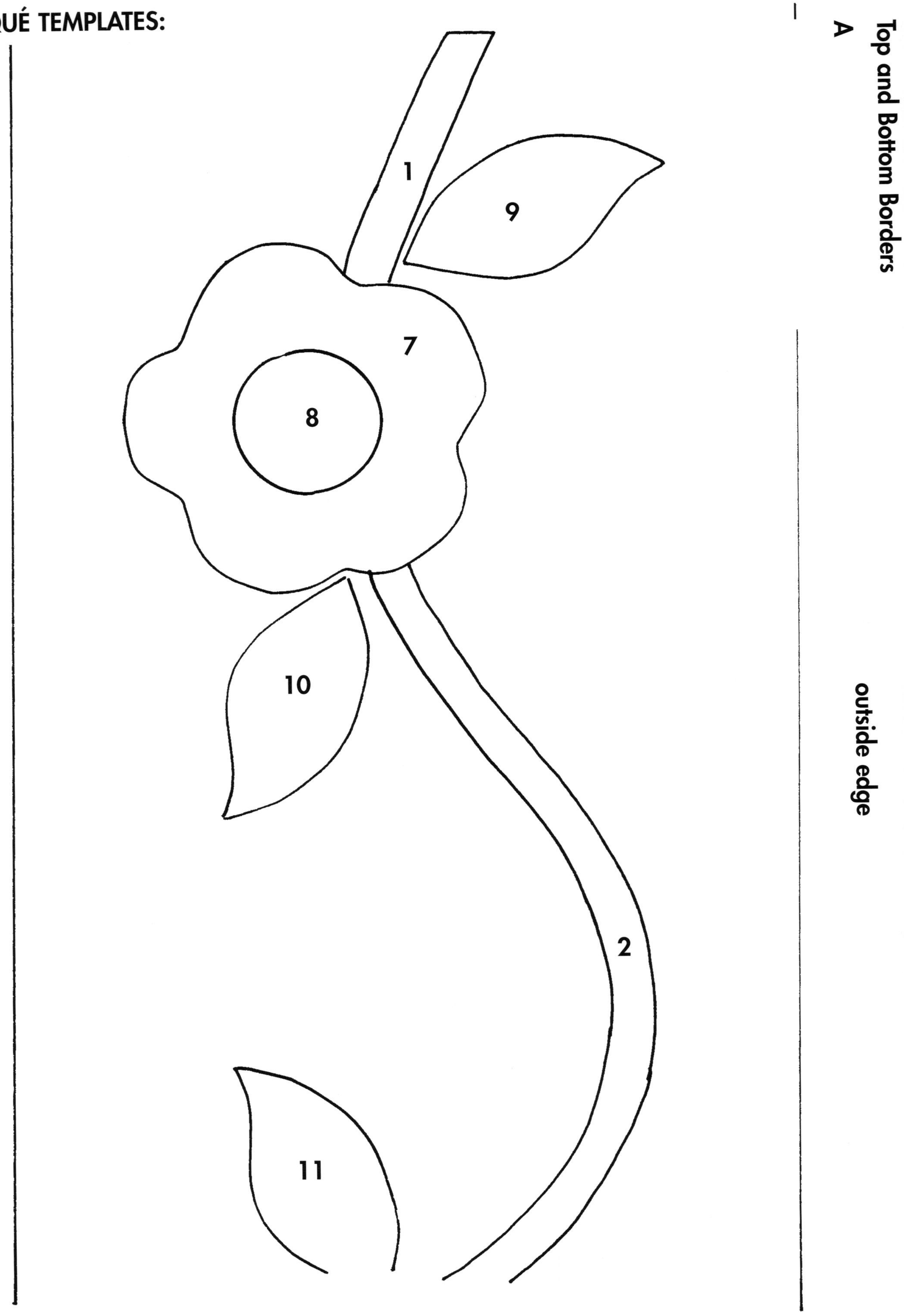

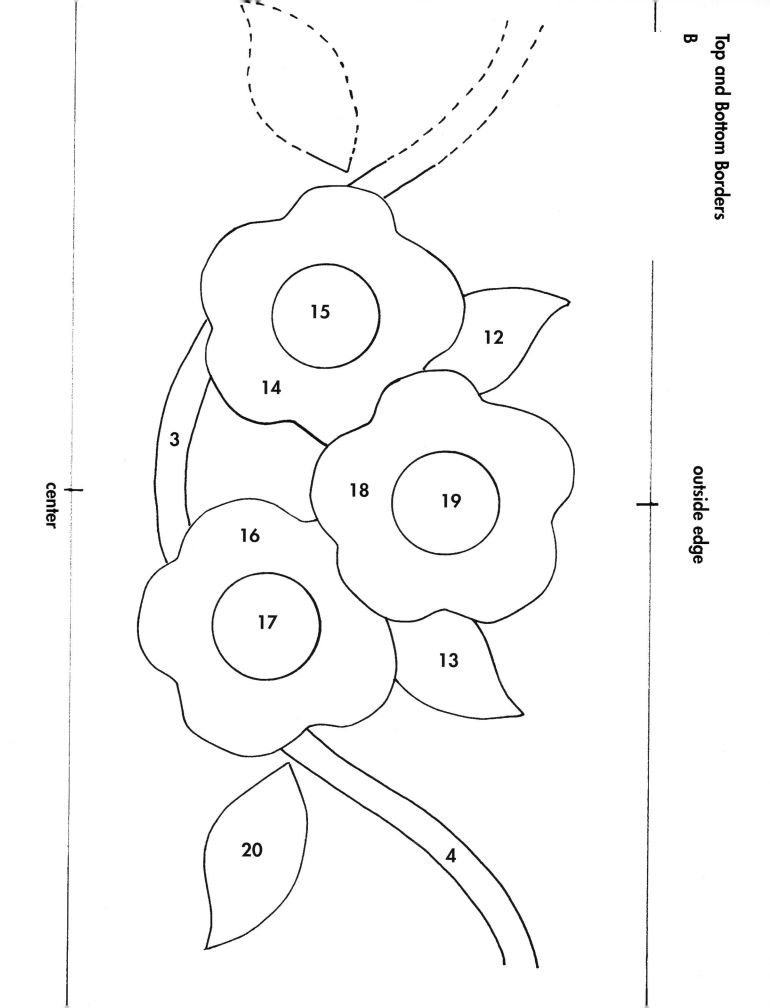

outside edge

center

outside edge

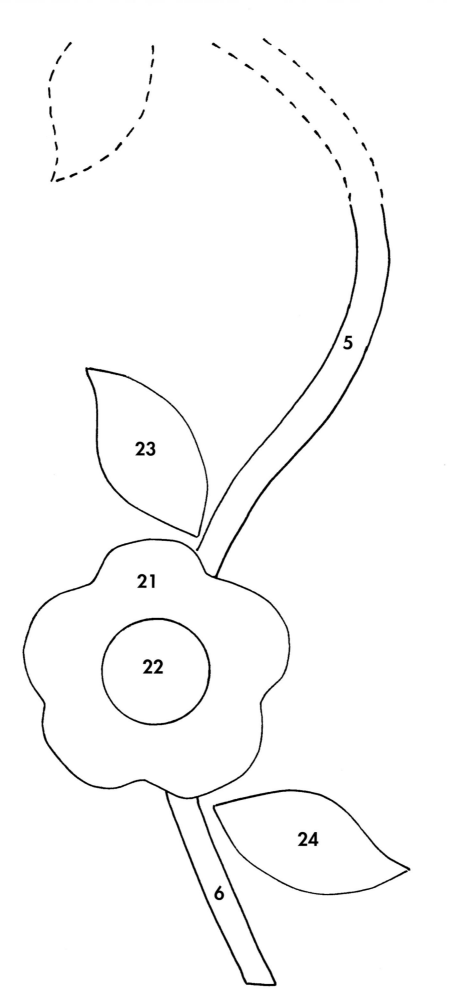

5

23

21

22

24

6

outside edge

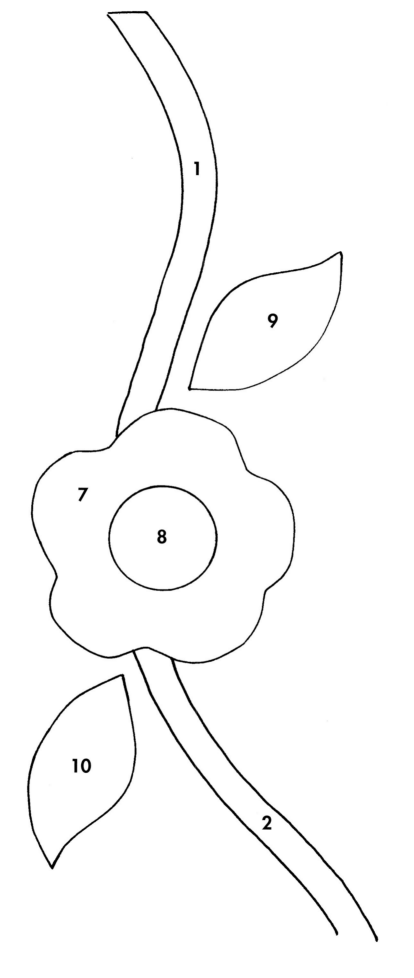

outside edge

center

3

14

11

21

22

19

20

4

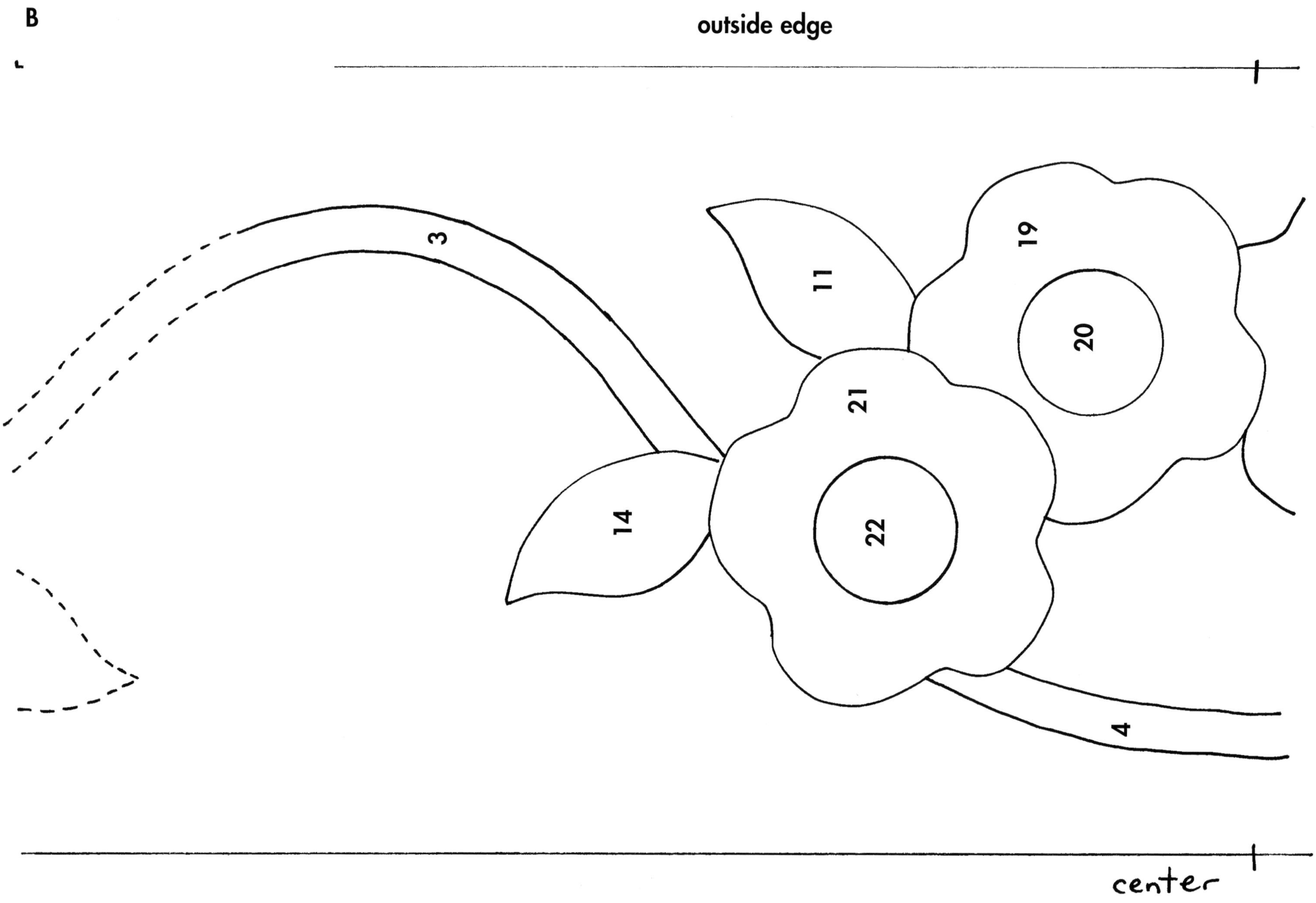

center

outside edge

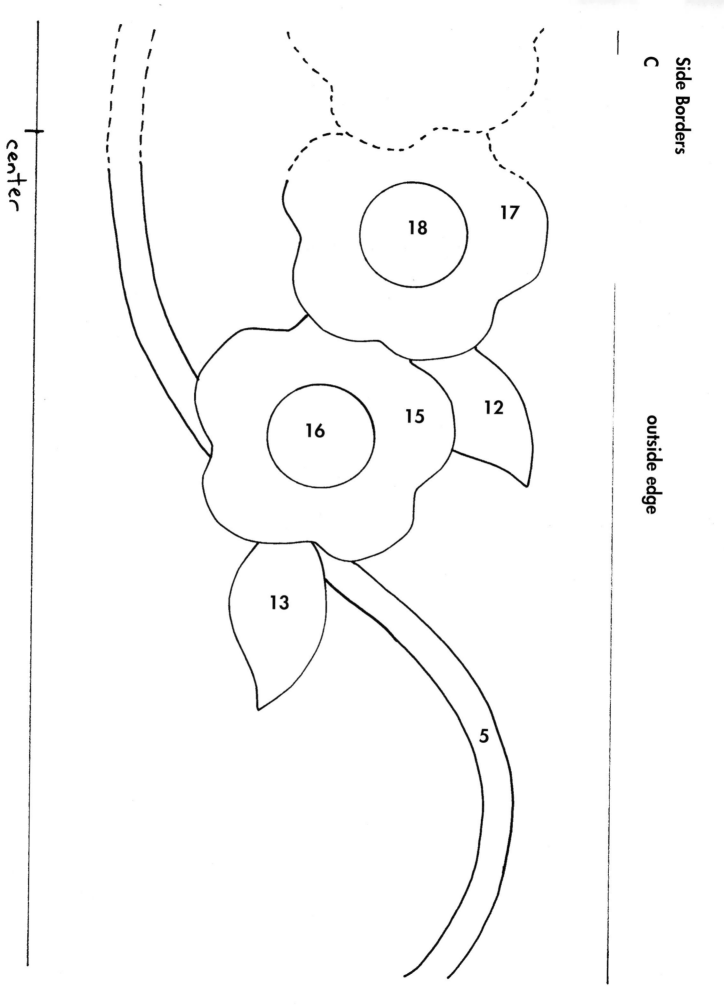

18

17

16

15

12

13

5

outside edge

25

23

24

26

6

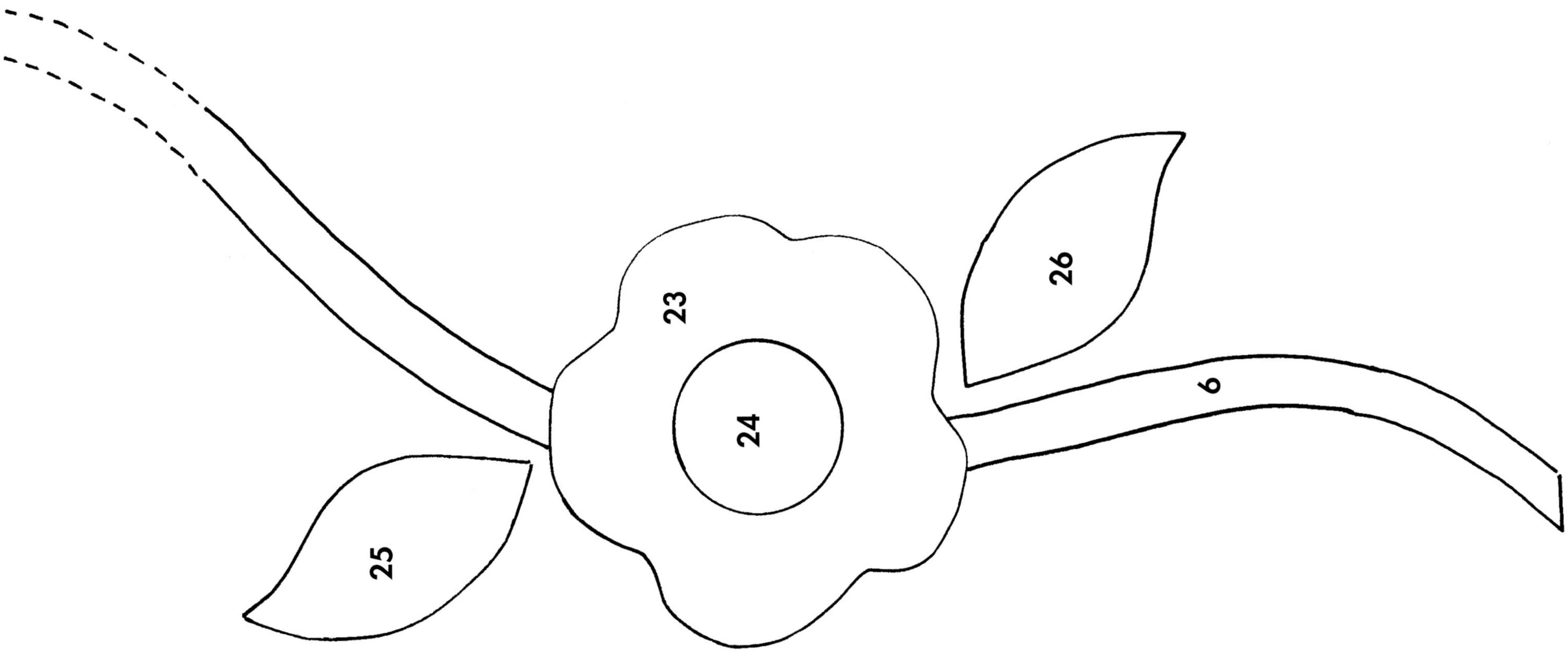

CORNER BLOCKS

RAILFENCE A BLOOMIN'

CHAPTER 7
THE GALLERY

"ANTIQUE DOUBLE NINE-PATCH"
47 1/2" x 60"
by Linda Mooney, Shawnee, KS from a pattern by Jeanne Poore, 2003

"CYNTHIA'S QUILT"

33" x 33"

by Linda Mooney, Shawnee, KS from a pattern by Jo Morton - Prairie Hand Patterns, 2001

142

"FLOWER GARDEN"
33" x 33"
by Lori Simpson, Olathe, KS, 2004

"SWEET MAGNOLIA"
18" x 18"
by Kathy Delaney, Overland Park, KS, 2003

"VARIABLE NINE PATCH #1"
21 1/2" x 21 1/2"
by Linda Mooney, Shawnee, KS, 2003

"VARIABLE NINE PATCH #2"
16 1/2" x 33"
by Linda Mooney, Shawnee, KS, 2003

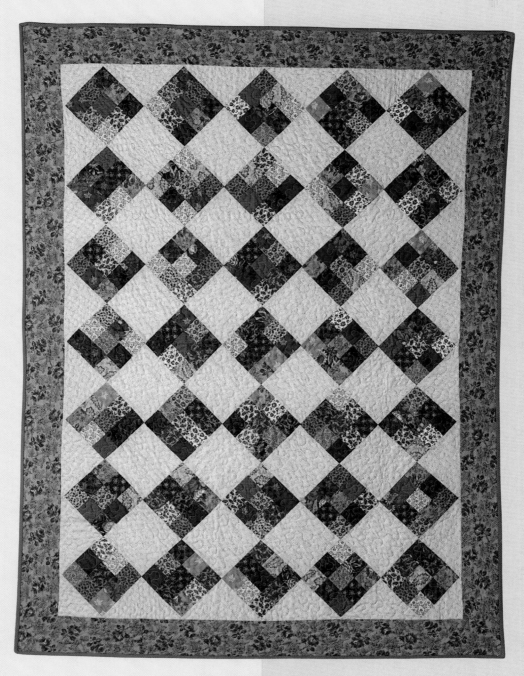

"FALL 9-PATCH"
49" x 66"
by Prairie Point Quilt shop staff, Shawnee, KS, 2002

"SARAH'S QUILT"
46 1/2" x 73"
by Sarah Alguire, age 15, Travis AFB, CA and Dorothy Kohout, Overland Park, KS,
quilted by Dick Kohout, 2004

148

"9-PATCH ALL AROUND"
Jacket by Linda Mooney, Shawnee, KS, 2004

149

You can find these other great Kansas City Star Quilt books at www.PickleDish.com:

Star Quilts XIV: Carolyn's Paper-Pieced Garden: Patterns for Miniature and Full-Sized Quilts

Star Quilts XV: Murders On Elderberry Road: Mystery Book

Star Quilts XVI: Friendships in Bloom: Round Robin Quilts

Star Quilts XVII: Baskets of Treasures: Designs Inspired by Life Along the River

Star Quilts XVIII: Heart & Home: Unique American Women and the Houses that Inspire

PROJECT BOOKS:

Santa's Parade of Nursery Rhymes

Fan Quilt Memories: A Selection of Fan Quilts from The Kansas City Star